TEXT RETRIEVAL SYSTEMS IN INFORMATION MANAGEMENT

TEXT RETRIEVAL SYSTEMS IN INFORMATION MANAGEMENT

G.G.Chowdhury
School of Information Studies for Africa
Addis Ababa

PUBLISHING FOR ONE WORLD
NEW AGE INTERNATIONAL (P) LIMITED, PUBLISHERS
New Delhi • Bangalore • Chennai • Cochin • Guwahati • Hyderabad
Jalandhar • Kolkata • Lucknow • Mumbai • Ranchi
Visit us at **www.newagepublishers.com**

Published by New Age International (P) Ltd., Publishers
First Edition: 1996
Reprint: 2009

Branches:

- 36, Malikarjuna Temple Street, Opp. ICWA, Basavanagudi, **Bangalore**. © (080) 26677815
- 26, Damodaran Street, T. Nagar, **Chennai**. © (044) 24353401
- Hemsen Complex, Mohd. Shah Road, Paltan Bazar, Near Starline Hotel, **Guwahati**. © (0361) 2543669
- No. 105, 1st Floor, Madhiray Kaveri Tower, 3-2-19, Azam Jahi Road, Nimboliadda, **Hyderabad**. © (040) 24652456
- RDB Chambers (Formerly Lotus Cinema) 106A,1st Floor, S.N. Banerjee Road, **Kolkata**. © (033) 22275247
- 16-A, Jopling Road, **Lucknow**. © (0522) 2209578
- 142C, Victor House, Ground Floor, N.M. Joshi Marg, Lower Parel, **Mumbai**. © (022) 24927869
- 22, Golden House, Daryaganj, **New Delhi**. © (011) 23262370, 23262368

ISBN: 978-81-224-0760-0

Rs. 195.00

C-09-02-3406

Printed in Ramprintographs, Delhi.
Typeset at Laser Print Craft, Delhi.

PUBLISHING FOR ONE WORLD
NEW AGE INTERNATIONAL (P) LIMITED, PUBLISHERS
4835/24, Ansari Road, Daryaganj, New Delhi-110002
Visit us at **www.newagepublishers.com**

To the loving memory of my father

Late A.G. Chowdhury

Preface

Primary objective of a library and/or information system can briefly be stated as the storage and retrieval of information. Libraries and information centres have been trying to achieve this objective over the years by devising more and more sophisticated methods for storage of information for its easy retrieval. Efforts have also been made to devising more and more improved techniques for efficient retrieval of information from a storage. These efforts got a tremendous impetus from the work of H.P. Luhn, who, more than 30 years ago, first applied computer in the storage and retrieval of information. This attempt was made to generate alphabetical index entries by using computers, and since then library and information professionals have been trying to make use of computers to meet their objectives, *i.e.*, for effective and efficient storage and retrieval of information.

Information handled by libraries and information centres, even today, is mostly textual, though other media of information, *viz.*, voice and image are also becoming common. Owing to the peculiar nature of textual information and typical nature of the requirements of the user, conventional software packages for database management operations are not suitable for information retrieval operations. Software, which are specially designed for the storage and manipulation of textual information, are called textual/text information management or text retrieval systems. These systems form the core area of study in this book. Experience shows that library and information professionals in the developing world, and India is no exception to this, are not so conversant with the software packages for textual information management. The most obvious questions that they face relate to—what is so special/peculiar about text retrieval systems, whether or not conventional database management software packages can be used for text retrieval operations, how to go about selecting a text retrieval software, what guidelines should be followed in such a task, and so on. This book addresses these issues.

Chapter 1 of the book sets the reader to the right path for the discussions in successive chapters. Basic issues related to information systems, information retrieval and library management operations, *etc.*, are addressed in it. The second Chapter attempts to orient the reader with the basic concepts and terminology of database systems. A brief introduction to the development of database technology through different generations will help readers understand, in a better way, the further discussions in the book. Chapter 3 provides an introduction to the basic concepts and issues of database management systems.

Major features and functions of text retrieval software are discussed in Chapter 4. Examples from some well-known text retrieval software have been chosen for illustration. Chapter 5 presents a brief discussion on the file structure of text retrieval systems. Guidelines for choosing a software, from among the large number of software packages available in the market, is provided in Chapter 6. Major steps for developing a text retrieval system have been discussed in Chapter 7. Chapter 8 presents an overview of some well-known text retrieval software packages.

Automation of library and information systems calls for the use of computers in text retrieval as well as in library house-keeping operations. While text retrieval systems differ widely from conventional database management operations, library management software, used for automating library house-keeping operations, closely resemble database management systems. Chapter 9 of this book provides a brief introduction to library management systems and highlights their major difference with text retrieval systems. A quick look at some of the text retrieval and library management software packages available in India, presented in Chapter 10, will help readers develop an idea of the prevailing situation.

Although all the text retrieval systems aim at retrieving information at the end of a search session, in reality what they come up with is either a list of sources where the user may subsequently find his required information, or part(s) of a text where the search term(s) appear. This has been a major criticism of all the text retrieval software. The other drawback of text retrieval systems relates to the user interface which is the gateway for the end-user to the stored information. Text retrieval software vary in accepting search expressions, particularly in case of complex search expressions where more than one search term need to be combined with various search operators. It is assumed that the end-user will be able to formulate his query by choosing all the appropriate search terms and then combining them by appropriate search operators. However, this does not happen always, *i.e.*, end-user may not be able to choose all the appropriate search terms, and moreover, they may not be able to prepare the most appropriate search expression by combining the search terms with the appropriate search operators.

Efforts to overcome this problem have given rise to a different kind of software for text retrieval, called the knowledge-based systems (KBS) or intelligent knowledge-based systems (IKBS). These systems employ techniques of expert systems, natural language processing, *etc.*, in order to make it possible for the end-user to interact with the system in natural language which would retrieve the actual information from the database rather than mere bibliographic references. A brief discussion on knowledge-based systems has been presented in Chapter 11. A quick look at some of the recent studies and research in different areas of information and text retrieval, presented in Chapter 12 of the book, will help readers get an idea of the future of text retrieval systems.

I am greatly indebted to Professor A. Neelameghan, a renowned information scientist and my former colleague at the School of Information Studies for Africa (SISA), for his valuable comments and suggestions on an earlier version of the manuscript of this book. This work would not have been possible without the constant support and help of my wife, Sudatta. She extended her support in many ways—in going through the manuscript and making valuable comments, in the tedious process of correcting the proof, and moreover, in keeping me away, as far as practicable, from the problems of day-to-day life.

I hope this book will be of use to the students and practising professionals in the field of library and information science.

G.G. Chowdhury
School of Information Studies for Africa (SISA)
Addis Ababa University
Addis Ababa, Ethiopia

October 1995

Contents

Chapter 1
Introduction

1.1 INFORMATION SYSTEMS

An Information system is an organisation of staff, materials, and equipment that is concerned with the functions of linking the sources and recipients of informative communication; telephone systems, consultancies, publishers, booksellers, libraries, database producers, database processors, etc., are the examples of information system[1]. According to a definition provided in a UNESCO report[2], information systems and services include:

- information and data in textual, factual, numerical and geographical representations, recorded in conventional or non-conventional media;
- information and data sources, systems, networks and services of different types including data banks, data bases, library systems and services, documentation centres and services, information clearing facilities, referral centres, information analysis, consolidation and repackaging centres and services; and
- information and data handling in conventional ways as well as through the application of modern information technologies.

Thus very simply one can say that information systems deal with information and data available in a variety of forms, and the basic function of an information centre is to store data in a way that is suitable for retrieving the same whenever required. The practical work of an information scientist is, therefore, concerned with the development, operation, and management of information systems of all kinds, and with all the various techniques and technologies by which information may be transferred[1].

From the connotation of information systems given above, we note that there are different kinds of organisations which can be called information systems, library systems being one example. Each kind of information system deals with some specific types of items or materials, and some specific techniques and technologies for manipulating information to attain one or more objectives. Focusing our attention towards library systems, we may note that there are two major groups of activities relating to the handling and dissemination of information, *viz.*,

— information retrieval operations, and
— housekeeping operations.

Both these sets of activities have been performed manually in libraries for centuries. The situation has changed significantly over the last three decades or so due to the introduction of computer and communication technologies for automation of different activities. Introduction of computer-based library systems have many advantages over the manual library systems and services.

1.2 REASONS FOR DEVELOPMENT OF COMPUTER-BASED LIBRARY SYSTEMS

Two main reasons for automation suited to all kinds of libraries are:

— to provide a service at lesser cost, and
— to provide added benefits at a lesser cost.

These points are too general and remind us about the ultimate goal of any system, that is, to provide the best possible service at the least cost. To make it somewhat generalised, we may note that new or improved services to library users and staff made possible with computer-based systems include:

— providing access to library's catalogue online, and
— allowing searches of vast amount of literature (information) in any subject field via online or on CD-ROM.

These are among many benefits of computer-based library systems. Some other reasons for the development of automated library systems may be mentioned as follows:

— to save money by avoiding duplication of jobs and by saving human labour;
— to provide a common system for libraries to merge, *i.e.*, to develop a ground for library cooperation and

resource-sharing;
- — to perform tasks more accurately, quickly and with increased control than with manual systems; and
- — to keep up pace with the growing demand of users and changing nature of services, and so on.

1.3 INFORMATION RETRIEVAL

A library usually performs a number of the following activities and services which come under the purview of information retrieval operations

- — cataloguing;
- — indexing;
- — current awareness service;
- — selective dissemination of information;
- — retrospective search service, *etc.*

Function of an information retrieval system is largely concerned with designing, implementing, and maintaining databases for effective and efficient retrieval of data/ information. One of the most important aspects of information retrieval concerns how the documents on a system are represented. The fastest computer or the most sophisticated search techniques cannot overcome the problems caused by poorly represented documents. There are potentially unlimited number of ways in which a given document can be represented in an information retrieval environment. The success of the retrieval system depends significantly on the way the documents in the database are represented.

Librarians and information professionals have been engaged in providing information retrieval services for quite a long time. Traditional methods of information retrieval services rely on manually-produced catalogue cards which provide access to the desired documents through some key values, such as, name of author, title of document, descriptors, etc. Users approach the catalogue with any of these keys and then identify the documents which may satisfy their information requirements.

Subject approach to information has long been met with the help of indexes of terms drawn from the title and/ or the text of the documents. Two broad categories of indexing systems evolved over the period of time, *viz.*, post-coordinate indexing and pre-coordinate indexing. In post-coordinate indexing systems, individual index terms are extracted and posted on cards and these are coordinated at the level of searching. Users are required to take out those cards whose index terms match their search terms, and then the cards are compared to determine the postings which are common to all the cards; the user then moves to the document collection with the corresponding document numbers for the information sought for.

In case of pre-coordinate systems, as the name suggests, index terms are coordinated at the time of preparing the index entries and thus users can get the full context in which a given search term occurs.

Both these systems of indexing rely on human expertise in generating index terms, drawing index entries, sorting and arranging the index cards, and then finally searching them in response to users' query. Thus, the whole process is enormously dependent on human intellectual capabilities.

With the advent of computers and their developments through generations—both in terms of hardware and software—computerised techniques for handling data and databases came up which are known as *database management systems.* However, these systems were, from the beginning, meant for handling those kinds of data which can be structured and the search mechanisms used to retrieve the database items are relatively straight forward. Owing to the peculiar nature of textual data which is basically unstructured and the search mechanisms are relatively complex, a different kind of database technology evolved over the period of time to handle specifically the textual data. These systems are known as *text retrieval systems;* they are meant for computerised storage and manipulation of textual data for different purposes of information retrieval.

While conventional manual information retrieval systems mostly store bibliographic information and searches are conducted on those bibliographic keys to retrieve the references where the actual information sought can be found, the automated text retrieval systems can handle both bibliographic information and the actual text (abstract or the full text). Thus users can either retrieve bibliographic references pertaining to an information search or can get access to the actual text stored in the database. When a text retrieval system deals with the full texts of documents it is called a *full text retrieval system.*

1.4 LIBRARY HOUSEKEEPING OPERATIONS

In addition to providing different information retrieval services through computer, the term library automation also refers to the application of computers in a number of housekeeping operations, such as,

- — acquisition;
- — circulation control;
- — serials control;
- — interlibrary loan;
- — resource sharing; *etc.*

Text retrieval systems are specifically designed for meeting the different needs of information retrieval services in libraries. Almost all the text retrieval packages available now-a-days are capable of providing facilities for the information retrieval services mentioned above. However, they are not usually meant for automating the library housekeeping operations. These issues are discussed later in this book.

1.5 REASONS FOR AUTOMATING LIBRARY HOUSE-KEEPING OPERATIONS

A question may often arise why should libraries go for automating their housekeeping operations, especially when some automated information retrieval services are available? There are many reasons for automating specific library procedures and functions which have been widely discussed in literature[3-8]. Some major reasons for automating such housekeeping operations as acquisition, circulation control, serials control, *etc.*, are mentioned in the following subsections.

1.5.1 Reasons for Developing Automated Circulation Control System

A circulation control system exists to

— record every loan of an item,
— provide information on items borrowed,
— make possible reservations and recalls, and
— cancel records for returned items.

In an automated system, these tasks along with others, *viz.*, preparation of various statistical reports, *etc.*, are done automatically.

Following points may be mentioned as some of the reasons for having an automated circulation control system. In other words, with an automated circulation control system we can achieve the following objectives:

1. Accurate and timely recording and maintenance of loan transaction data;
2. Accurate, timely, and thorough handling of overdues, fines and other exception conditions;
3. Recording of and access to status and other information about the collection, for example, on loan, overdue, lost, *etc.;*
4. Reduction in staff time devoted to circulation functions;
5. Increase in speed and efficiency of service to users;
6. Reduction in work load to manage reserve collections;
7. Efficient maintenance of borrower records;
8. Provision of accurate, reliable and timely statistics relating to issue, return, *etc.;*
9. Evaluation of library materials on the basis of usage statistics; and
10. Interaction with interlibrary loans for improved access.

1.5.2 Reasons for Developing Automated Acquisition System

An acquisition system is concerned with book identification, ordering, receiving and accessioning. A large number of tasks must be carried out after the initial receipt of a book suggestion. In addition, it is sometimes necessary to assemble information, such as, number of books on order, value of fund, *etc.* An automated acquisition system helps to achieve the following objectives:

1. automatic check-up of requested/recommended items with the existing stock of the library for avoiding duplication;
2. automatic generation of order notes;
3. maintaining details of items on order;
4. generating claims for items ordered but not received;
5. maintaining accounts;
6. maintaining records and performance figures of vendors;
7. accessioning the items on arrival;
8. generation of various statistics; *etc.*

1.5.3 Reasons for Developing Automated Serials Control system

A serials control system is designed to serve a number of functions, *viz.*,

— procurement of serials;
— renewal of subscriptions;
— generation of reminders for non-receipt issues;
— controlling the budget regarding the subscription; and
— maintaining various statistics.

There are many advantages of having a serials control system automated. The following objectives may be achieved with an automated serials control system:

1. automatic selection of suitable titles for procurement;
2. automatic generation of purchase orders;
3. proper organisation of financial matters and charging the appropriate account;
4. automatic generation of claim letters for issues not received within due time;
5. keeping current details of serials holdings;
6. providing access to details of current holdings;
7. allowing individual issues to be routed to various members of the organisation;
8. allowing journals to be borrowed by the members;
9. organisation of the binding job;
10. producing various statistics and management information like money spent for each department/section for purchase of journals over a period of time.

number and list of journals subscribed by each department/section, trend of increase in the cost of journals over a period of time; and so on.

1.6 NEED FOR BOTH THE DBMS AND TEXT RETRIEVAL SYSTEMS

Both Database Management System (DBMS) and Text Retrieval software packages support the management of and retrieval from collections of shared data. A DBMS is a software system which is designed for the organisation and maintenance of databases, with provisions for maintaining security, reliability and integrity. Text retrieval systems deal with unstructured data; it is a system that accepts, collates and stores texts from a variety of sources, retrieves specific information from the text in response to queries, and processes the retrieved text in a user-defined format.

In a library, both the aspects of database management and text retrieval operations are needed. For example, in a circulation control system, information is to be extracted from more than one file (document file, borrower file, loan file, *etc.*); the activities thus resemble to typical database management operations. Cataloguing, indexing, etc., on the other hand, exemplify typical text retrieval operations.

This book aims to discuss the basic concepts of both the text retrieval and database management systems, along with their differences, in the context of libraries. However, it should be noted that the boundaries between library management systems, text retrieval systems, and database management systems have been eroded over the past few years so that if the central requirement is for a database application, packages from all of these three categories must be examined and compared[9]. The final selection of a suitable software may be determined by the quality of the database software, but often it will be determined by subsidiary requirements, for say, indexing or circulation control.

1.7 CONCEPT RETRIEVAL

Conventional text/information retrieval systems mainly rely on term-based approach, *i.e.*, appropriate search terms are generated from users' queries and mechanisms are provided in the text retrieval systems to retrieve the records where the search term(s) occur. Thus unless an efficient mechanism is provided for indexing and searching the text databases, the resulting output may not always be upto the users' satisfaction. The basic reason for this is that users actually look for certain concept(s) rather than individual terms; documents retrieved by simple term matching merely contain the search terms but the content of the documents may be conceptually different from that the user is looking for.

Need for a conceptual approach for retrieving information was, however, felt by library and information science professionals quite a long time ago. As a result a number of pre-coordinate indexing systems were developed which basically attempt to represent the indexed documents conceptually. Examples of such indexing systems are

— Chain Indexing of S.R. Ranganathan,
— Relational Indexing of J.E.L. Farradane,
— PRECIS (PREserved Context Index System) of D. Austin,
— POPSI (POstulate-based Permuted Subject Indexing) of G. Bhattacharyya, and so on.

Fundamental mechanisms of each of these systems comprise analysis of the given texts with a view to generate a conceptual representation of the contents of the documents; index entries are generated from this conceptual representation based on certain rules provided in each indexing system. Similar conceptual representation of users' queries may be prepared and be matched with the index entries thereby retrieving those items which are conceptually equivalent.

These systems of information retrieval were originally practised manually, and later, with the availability of computers, some semi-automatic methods were developed. The major part, that is, the analysis and interpretation of the document texts and thus generation of the conceptual representation remained manual, while methods for generating index entries under each approach term, and alphabetical arrangement of the index entries have been made automatic. The first part could not be easily automated because this is a highly intellectual job and, therefore, it is difficult to be generalised and to generate strict rules for the purpose. Generation of index entries and their sorting is, however, a more routine job and, therefore, could be automated easily.

These manual information retrieval systems have faced two major criticisms:

First, the process is highly human-dependent. Result of analysis and interpretation of a given text and thus the resulting conceptual representation is dependent on the indexer's ability, subject knowledge and expertise. Thus the system is prone to inaccuracy and inconsistency, and is very much subjective—it is often noted that if two indexers are asked to prepare index entries for the same document, there is a very high probability that the resulting conceptual representation will differ from one another.

The *second* point of criticism relates to the degree of abstraction. By asking an indexer to produce a statement that would conceptually represent a given document, we mean to represent the intellectual content of the document in a single sentence or statement. This may obviously cause loss of information; the author of the text might have used hundreds or thousand of sentences to express the thought content, while the indexer is asked to express the same by only one sentence or sentence-like phrase.

These problems of manual conceptual information retrieval systems forced researchers to go for automation and to look for suitable methods for the purpose. This gave rise to an emerging area of study and research in the field of automated text/information retrieval systems—the knowledge-based systems which encompass various advanced areas of research like natural language processing, expert systems, *etc.*

1.8. ORGANISATION OF THE BOOK

This book covers various aspects of text retrieval systems and related systems in its Chapters 4, 5, 6, and 7, whereas aspects of library management systems are discussed in Chapters 9 and 10. However, in order to facilitate these discussions, Chapter 2 describes some basic issues of database technology in general, and development in database management technology. Similarly, Chapter 3 discusses some elementary concepts of database management systems, relational database management systems, and recent trends of study and research in different areas of database management systems, namely, multimedia database systems, distributed database systems, and object-oriented database management systems.

Chapter 4 discusses different aspects of text retrieval systems in detail. In order to understand text retrieval operations one is required to have some idea about the ways different files are handled. Chapter 5 describes some file-handling techniques used in text retrieval operations. Library and information professionals often find it difficult to pick up the most suitable package from among the many available in the market. Chapter 6 provides guidelines for choosing a text retrieval software.

Once a software is chosen, the next task is to go ahead with the development of a text retrieval system. However, there are a number of considerations involved and a number of specific steps are to be followed. These points are discussed in Chapter 7. Chapter 8 briefly presents the features of six widely-known text retrieval software packages.

Software which have been designed to handle house-keeping operations in libraries are known as library management software. Chapter 9 discusses some aspects of library management systems. The Indian scenario with regard to text retrieval and library management software is discussed in Chapter 10. Chapter 11 of the book provides an introduction to knowledge-based systems and discusses applicability of such systems in various library operations. Chapter 12 presents an overview of the recent studies and research in different areas of information and text retrieval.

REFERENCES

1. Brian Vickery and Alina Vickery, *Information Science in Theory and Practice*, London, Butterworth, 1987.

2. A. Neelameghan and J. Tocatlian, Egypt, National Information Policy, Establishment of a National Information Policy and Strategy for its Implementation, Paris, UNESCO, 1987 (RP/1986-1987/VII. 2. 1). (FMR/ PGI/103).
3. N. Higham, Computer Needs for University Library Operations: a Report, Standing Conference of National and University Libraries, UK, 1973.
4. D. Reynolds, *Library Automation: Issues and Applications*, New York, R.R. Bowker, 1985.
5. L.A. Tedd, *An Introduction to Computer-based Library Systems*, Ed. 3, Chichester, John Wiley, 1993.
6. P. Gillman and S. Peniston, *Library Automation: A Current Review*, London, Aslib, 1984.
7. P.F. Burton and J.H. Petrie, *The Librarian's guide to Microcomputers for Information Management*, Van Nostrand Reinhold, 1986.
8. J. Leeves, *Library Systems: a Buyer's Guide*, Ed. 2, Aldershot, Gower, 1989.
9. J.E. Rowley, Guidelines on the Evaluation and Selection of Library Software Packages, *Aslib Proceedings*, Vol. 42, No. 9, 1990, 225-235.
10. W. Saffady, *Text Storage and Retrieval Systems: a Technology Survey and Product Directory* London, Meckler, 1989.
11. M.E. Williams, *The State of Databases Today, In: 'Computer-readable databases: a Directory and Data Sourcebook*, ed. by K.Y. Marcaccio, Detroit, Michigan, Gale Research Inc., 1989, vii-xiv.
12. H. Dyer and A. Gunson, *A Directory of Library and Information Retrieval Software for Microcomputers*, Ed. 4, Aldershot, Gower, 1990.
13. R. Kimberley, ed., *Text Retrieval: a Directory of Software*, Ed 3, Aldershot, Gower, 1990.
14. J.R. Matthews, *Choosing an Automated Library System: a Planning Guide*, Chicago, American Library Association, 1980.
15. J. Beaumont and D. Krueger, eds., *Microcomputers for Libraries: How Useful are they?* Canadian Library Association. Ottawa, 1983.

16. W.R. Converse, Microcomputers in Academic Libraries: Current Applications and Future Impact, In: The Application of Micro-Computer in Information, Documentation and Libraries, Vol. 4, ed., by K.D. Lehmann and H. Strohl-Goebel, North-Holland, Elsevier Science Publishers, 1987, 83-90.
17. J. Rowley, *Computers for Libraries*, Ed. 3. London, Library Association, 1993.

Chapter 2
Database Technology

2.1 INTRODUCTION

Database technology emerged in the late sixties as a result of a combination of various circumstances. There was a growing demand among users for more information to be provided by the computer relating to the day-to-day running of the organisation as well as to information for planning and control purposes. This demand coincided with advances in computer technology and in expertise in computer data processing. The technology that emerged to process and manipulate data of various kinds is grossly termed as database management technology, and the resulting software are known as database management systems (DBMSs). DBMSs do just what the name suggests, *i.e.*, They manage a computer-stored database or collection of data. In the next few sections we are going to discuss the basic concepts of database systems, their growth and recent trends of research in database technology.

2.2 DATA

The word data refers to a set of given facts. Information in a form which can be processed by a computer is called data. Data has for long been used to refer to scientific measurements, but words constitute data just as numbers. A list of names is data, a set of keywords is data, a doctor's record of his patients is data, and figures relating to temperature, humidity, *etc.*, or sales of a company, are data.

2.3 DATABASE

A database can be conceived as a system whose base, whose key concept, is simply a particular way of handling data. In other words, a database is nothing more than a computer-based record keeping system[1]. The overall objective of a database is to record and maintain information.

The Macmillan Dictionary of Information Technology[2] defines a database as a collection of interrelated data stored so that it may be accessed by authorised users with simple user-friendly dialogues. *The Chambers Science and Technology Dictionary*[3] provides a more simple definition of a database—a collection of structured data independent of any particular application.

It may be noted from the above two definitions that a database contains some data which are structured and integrated. Ellingen[4] defines a database as a collection of information that can be searched as a single entity. According to Oxborrow[5] a database can be considered as an organised collection of related sets of data, managed in such a way as to enable the user or application program to view the complete collection, or a logical subset of the collection, as a single unit.

From the above definitions we can simplify the definition of a database as—an organised collection of related sets of data which can be accessed by more than one user by simple means and can be searched to reveal those that touch upon a particular need.

In the computer world we frequently deal with files which are the outer identifying boundary or a sort of folder containing data. Thus a file is equivalent to an ordinary address book, if we are talking about names and addresses. A file in a computer is given a unique name by which it is addressed.

2.4 RECORDS AND FIELDS

A record is a collection of information that is all related[4]. A database is an organised collection of units of information, and each unit of information in a database is called a record. A record is generally what a user wants to find while searching a database. An example of a record is a book card in a library's catalogue, which describes the book's title, author, subject, etc. A collection of database records constitutes a database file[6]. Identifying what is to be the record is one of the early tasks in designing a database. If the database is a bibliographic one, the bibliographic information about each document is the unit of information or record.

A stored record is a named-collection of associated stored fields[7]. Each record is made up of particular segment or element of information which is called field. A field holds a particular type of information within a record that can be separately addressed. The different items of information in a bibliographic record may be author, title, *etc.* Thus the different fields in a bibliographic record can be 'author field' containing name(s) of author(s), 'title field' containing the title, and so on. A field may be subdivided into still smaller units called sub fields. For example, if 'imprint' is regarded as a field in a bibliographic database, then the different components of imprint, *viz.*, publisher's name, place of publication, and date of publication, can be called subfields.

A record is thus composed of fields and subfields. Identifying what fields and subfields are to be included in each record is an important task in the database design procedure. Each field is given a unique identifier, called 'Field Tag', at the design stage, which is then used throughout for data input, editing, searching, printing, *etc.*

2.5 PROPERTIES OF DATABASES

A database is designed to avoid duplication of data as well as to permit retrieval of information to satisfy a wide variety of user information needs[8]. The major properties of a database can be summarised as follows[9]:

- It is integrated with provisions for different applications;
- It eliminates or reduces data duplication;
- It enhances data independence by permitting application programs to be insensitive to changes in the database;
- It permits shared access;
- It permits finer granularity;
- It provides facilities for centralised control of accessing and security control functions.

2.6 KINDS OF DATABASES

In discussing databases it is sometimes useful to classify them by the type of data record contained and sometimes by subject coverage. The two major divisions are: reference databases and source databases. Reference databases lead the users to the source of the information: a document, person or organisation. Source databases provide the answer with no need to refer elsewhere[10].

Reference databases may be divided into two broad groups— bibliographic databases and referral databases. Bibliograhic databases contain bibliographic information, sometimes associated with abstracts, and allow users to search through bibliographic keys, like author, title, keyword, *etc.* Referral databases contain details and addresses of useful persons, organisations or of research projects; the objective is to direct the users to persons or organisations for a particular item of information. Bibliographic databases may be classified according to subject, *e.g.*, chemical databases; according to types of documents, *e.g.*, patent databases, and so on.

Source databases may be categorised as numeric, *e.g.*, statistical databases, text-numeric, *e.g.*, company annual report databases, or full-text databases containing full-texts of documents. A text storage and retrieval system—variously termed as text retrieval system, full-text retrieval system, text information management system or a text data management system—is a computer-based information storage and retrieval system which stores the textual contents of documents in machine-readable form for retrieval or other kind of processing by computer.

2.7 DATABASE INDEXING

When data is added to a database, the most important decision to be taken is—how the data elements will be indexed. Indexing determines the capability of the system to retrieve information from the database.

Different approaches to indexing can be adopted. Word or term indexing is by far the most commonly used form of indexing. 'Every word indexing' implies that an index exists for every word in a designated field. Here the user can choose any word for searching the database. Positional information is quite useful for word indexing. This is required for conducting proximity/adjacency searching. For example, user may want that the word 'retrieval' should be preceded by 'information' in the data (as in 'information retrieval'). Dates can be indexed in a number of different ways.

The overhead or disk space can be reduced by using a stopwords list. Stopwords are the words that one does not want to index, or in other words, which are not potential search terms. Most commonly used stopwords list include insignificant words like A, AN, AND, BY, FOR, FROM, IN, OF, ON, THE, *etc.*

Once the indexes are created, the next question comes is their storage. For a large database, the number of index terms will be huge and, therefore, proper decisions are to be taken for their storage. Proper storage of index terms saves overhead space and also facilitates fast searching.

Different methods of indexing have evolved over the period of time for efficient handling of data. As far as text retrieval is concerned, by far the most used indexing is the inverted file which is a straight alphabetical list of index terms with pointers to records. Different methods of organising inverted files are there, but the most used one is the B-tree and alphabetic chain. Other methods of organising textual information are hashing, text signature *etc.* These methods are discussed in Chapter 5 of this book.

2.8 DATABASE SEARCHING

There are two basic methods for searching a database, *viz.*, combinatorial searching and iterative searching. In combinatorial searching, searches are conducted for each index term and then those are combined to find out the common pointer(s). This is the primary way in which DIALOG searching is done.[4] The advantage of this method is that any form of combination of search terms can be chosen. The disadvantage is that one must consume additional time to search the entire database with each set.

In iterative searching, search is conducted successively on a diminishing set size. At the outset search is conducted to get the largest set, and then next search is conducted on that set. For example, in order to get 'items on librarianship published by the UNESCO between 1985-1990', the steps may be as follows:

- — first get the set of items on librarianship;
- — at the next stage, conduct a search on that set to get only those published by UNESCO, and
- — conduct a further search on the retrieved set with date of publication.

The advantage of this search is that the database can be searched more quickly, since searches are conducted on a constantly narrowing number of records.

2.9 GROWTH OF DATABASE TECHNOLOGY

The historical development of database technology has been closely related to the development of computer hardware and software. With respect to hardware development, it is now common to talk about 'computer generations', and in a similar way several 'database system generations' can be distinguished.

The history of database systems to date can be divided into five generations which roughly follow five decades of computing that started with the 1950s, the first two of which were concerned with predecessors of database systems.[11] A central role in this development was played by the ongoing evolution of hardware and software, on the one hand, and a continuous change and increase in the user requirements for data processing, on the other.

The *first generation* concerns the 1950s. In these early days, the major task of any computer system was to process data under the control of a program which primarily meant calculating, counting, and so on. Each individual program was either directly provided with the data set it operated upon, or it read its data from some secondary memory into the main memory of the computer, processed it and finally wrote the modified set back to the secondary memory. Secondary memory then referred to punched cards or to magnetic tapes, both of which allowed sequential processing only. Thus the first file systems exclusively allowed a sequential access to the records of a file.

The *second generation* (the early sixties) was different from the first one in several aspects. On the one hand, it became possible to use computers in dialogue mode as well as batch mode. On the other hand, the development of magnetic disks as fast secondary memory led to the arrival of more sophisticated file systems which now rendered multiple access possible. A direct access file allows access to a record in that file directory via its address (on the disk), which are physically located in front of it. Such an address can be located, for example, in a special index file, or found by using a hash function.

Both the generations were thus characterised by the availability of file systems only, which strictly speaking are the forerunners of database systems. Of prime importance for the use of a file system is the static association of certain data sets (files) with individual programs which operate on these. As an example, consider a library which stores data on books it owns, on the readers who may use the library, and on books which are currently checked out. In this case, all possible events (recording of new acquisitions, *etc.*) are handled by particular program where each program is provided with a copy of the files it needs for the appropriate time period. Thus individual files must exist in multiple copies, since in general all events occur overlapped in time and are hence processed in parallel. In addition, if the programs are written by distinct programmers, it might be difficult to enforce a uniform formatting when the individual files are being created. It is obvious that there will be problems of redundancy, inconsistency, inflexibility, *etc.*

The *third generation*, which roughly coincides with the 1970s but actually started in the late sixties, is characterised by the introduction of a distinction between logical and physical information, which occurred parallel to an increasing need to manage large collections of data. During that time data models were used for the first time to describe physical structures from a logical point of view. However, the then emerging approaches such as the hierarchical or the network model have to be classified as 'implementation-oriented'.[11]

Starting from this distinction between the logical meaning of data, that is, the syntax and semantics of its description, and its current physical value, systems were developed which could integrate all the data of a given application into one collection with only a particular 'view' to it.

The *fourth generation*, which generally reached the market place in the 1980s saw systems, now called DBMSs, which in addition to storing data redundancy free under a centralised control make a clear distinction between a physical and a logical data model, which is particularly true for the relational model of data. Systems based on this model are typically provided with a high degree of physical data independence and the availability of powerful languages. The former aspect means that any physical storing of data is transparent ('invisible') to the users, and that in principle both the physical and logical side be changed without the other side being affected. The latter aspect primarily results from a transaction from record-oriented to set-oriented management and processing of the data in a database. The language which users have for working with a relational system considerably frees them from questions of 'how' to manage data; they may instead concentrate on the 'what'.

While the third generation may be termed 'pre-relational' and the fourth 'relational', it can be expected that the *fifth generation*, which is beginning to emerge for the 1990s, will be termed 'post-relational'.[11] The most significant achievement of this generation are the object-oriented database systems, multimedia systems and knowledge-based systems. Tremendous amount of research efforts are now devoted to these areas all over the world.

REFERENCES

1. Rose Deakin, *The Database Primer*, London, Century Pub., 1983.
2. D. Langley and M. Shain, eds., *Macmillan Dictionary of Science and Technology*, Ed. 2, London, Macmillan, 1985.

3. P.M.B. Walker, *Chambers Science and Technology Dictionary*, Cambridge, Chambers, 1988.
4. D.C. Ellingen, Database Design, *Database*, Vol. 14, No. 3, 1991, 104-106.
5. E. Oxborrow, *Databases and database management systems: concepts and issues*, Ed., 2, Chichester, Chartwell-Bratt, 1989.
6. Betty Eddison, Database Design, *Database*, April 1989, 88-90.
7. C.J. Date, *An Introduction to Database Systems*, Ed. 3, Reading MA, Addison-Wesley, 1981.
8. E.M. Cortez and E. J. Kazlauskas, *Managing Information Systems and Technologies: a Basic Guide for Design, Selection, Evaluation and Use*, New York, Neal-Schuman Pub. Inc. 1986.
9. B.G. Claybrook, *File Management Techniques*, New York, John Wiley, 1983.
10. P. Gillman and S. Peniston, *Library Automation: a Current Review*. London, Aslib, 1984.
11. Gottfried Vossen, *Data models, database languages and database management systems*. Wokingham, England, Addison-Wesley Pub. Co., 1991.
12. J.F. Courtney and D.B. Paradice, *Database Systems for Management* St. Louis, Times Mirror, 1988.

Chapter 3

Database Management Systems: Basic Concepts

3.1 INTRODUCTION

Database management systems (DBMS) do just what the name suggests, *i.e.*, they manage a computer-stored database or collection of data. DBMSs were originally developed for large computers to assist with the development, implementation and maintenance of related computer systems.[1] A DBMS is a software designed to make it possible to store and retrieve information in a database. Eastman[2] identifies a DBMS as a software package that is designed to facilitate the management of integrated data.

According to Claybrook[3], a DBMS can be defined as a large piece of software running on top of an operating system that accesses a database. Rumble[4] defines a database management system as the computer software and associated documentation that

— manage and maintain database(s);
— permit many users to use the same data regardless of storage considerations; and
— organise data items in a pre-defined or "logical" manner.

Oxborrow[5] defines a DBMS as a system which facilitates shared access to data in a database, and which maintains the reliability, security and integrity of the database by controlling access to it and supervising updates.

A close look through the above definitions reveal that a DBMS is a software which is designed for the organisation and maintenance of databases with provisions for maintaining security, reliability and integrity. Salton[6] thus mentions that DBMSs usually

— create and manipulate files;
— ensure smooth interactions between the user and the

file system through special file processing languages and control procedures;

— maintain data correctness and consistency using the available syntactic and semantic definitions of the data;

— provide appropriate file organisations for the stored data; and

— preserve the integrity and security of the file system in case of errors and breakdowns.

A DBMS thus is interposed between users and the stored files. The file structure in a DBMS is usually represented in a schema. A high-level data definition language (DDL) is used to specify the file schema. A data manipulation language (DML) is used to access and manipulate the files. Stored data dictionaries and physical file specifications are used to translate the statements in high-level data definition and data manipulation languages into actual file operations. The physical data independence is ensured by the fact that the physical file arrangement can be altered without affecting the user's application programs.[6]

3.2 AIMS OF DBMSs

Although DBMSs handle the task of information retrieval, they are different from the conventional information retrieval software. DBMSs were developed to handle formatted data used in the operation of an enterprise; information retrieval systems originated to provide bibliographic and numeric information service, and were originally meant to handle unstructured data. However, day-by-day both the functional and environmental lines are becoming blurred.[2]

The basic objectives of a DBMS relate to

— shared access to databases;

— maintenance of databases;

— control over data correctness, consistency, integrity and security, *etc.*

Kemp[7] identifies the following nine major aims of a DBMS:

— to avoid unnecessary duplication of data;

— to ensure data consistency;

— to enable rapid updating;

— to facilitate concurrent use of a database by more than one user;
— to increase control over data;
— to increase security of data;
— to achieve independence between programs and data;
— to reduce need for program alterations; and
— to facilitate maintenance of standards.

3.3 BASIC FEATURES OF DBMSs

A DBMS has a number of features, some of which are as follows:[8]

— Information is held in a number of 'record' types, often grouped in hierarchies, which reflect both the inherent structure of the data and the access paths which users will need to follow to find and manipulate the information; the overall structure is a 'schema'.
— Each user may have an independent 'view' of the database, selecting subsets of records and their component fields, and having this presented in 'user-adapted' format; this may be called a 'sub-schema'.
— The information structure of the whole database, enclosing all user views, is defined in a data dictionary, which forms a reference file about data and processes in the system, and provides a means of maintaining strict control on content and usage.
— The DBMS maintains the relationship between various record types, and the associated pointers, indexes and chains. It also copes with storage of variable length records when necessary, and if the designer has made a good job of the structure, offers fast access to the data for presentation, manipulation and updating.
— The DBMS may also be expected to 'log' the transactions being performed, and to set restart markers, so that recovery from system failure is fast and robust; this facility may occupy a major part of the program code involved in developing a DBMS package.
— Operation in a DBMS usually needs no programming.
— They are simple to set up and use.

— They are menu- as well as command-driven.

Salton and McGill[9] suggest that the following features are present in most database management implementations and these features render such systems attractive to user population:

1. The user programs exhibit *physical data independence* because they do not depend on the actual implementation methods used by the concerned database management system.
2. User programs may effectively be independent of the internal structure of the database objects and of the various relationships which may be defined between objects.
3. Users are provided with high level language facilities for submission of queries to the system and for specifying the required file processing operations.
4. Users may supply validation statements concerning the characteristics of files and data items thereby letting the system automatically provide error checks designed to verify the validation assertations.
5. In the event of accidental failure, restart facilities are provided which is charged with maintaining correct processing sequence.
6. Security provisions are available which ensure that the stored information is not misused or misappropriated.

3.4 SUMMARY OF MAIN DBMS FACILITIES

Oxborrow[5] identifies seven sets of facilities available in all the available DBMS packages. These are:

1. Data description
   — Record/relation, *etc.*, description;
   — Structured data description;
   — View (subschema) description.
2. Data input/edit/update
   — File-based;
   — Interactive/form-based.
3. Data retrieval
   — Interactive query language;
   — Other data retrieval/manipulation language.

4. General purpose data manipulation—application programming facilities via host language, or self-contained language.
5. Data presentation
   — Tabular display of results;
   — Report facilities;
   — Graphical display.
6. Database protection
   — Passwords/authorisation rules;
   — Backup copy/transaction logs;
   — Validation rule and concurrent access locks and rules.
7. Data administration
   — Integrated data dictionary;
   — Usage monitoring;
   — Physical organisation facilities (indexing/hashing/sorting/file characteristics, *etc.*).

3.5 FUNCTIONS OF DBMSs

Claybrook[3] defines a DBMS as a software that facilitates the use and control of large information files normally maintained on external storage devices, and includes the ability of a data description/definition language (DDL) and a data manipulation language (DML). The language used to define the logical structure of database is called DDL; it can be used to define the data items and their interrelationships. A language used to access the data in a database is called the DML; it is used to perform insertions, deletions, updates and retrievals. A DML can be defined as an extension to a host programming language, such as COBOL, or Pascal, or as a self-contained language; in the latter case it is often known as a query language. A DBMS may provide both the host and query language facilities. In addition, facilities are provided for database administration which include handling security, monitoring performance, backup and recovery. The main functions of a database management system can thus be described as follows:

1. **Integration:** Data integration denotes the utility to ensure that data items need not be

duplicated when additional applications call for their use. The integration facility ensures that whenever a particular item is changed or updated, the change is recognised throughout the system.

2. **Data independence:** DBMSs provide facilities for separation of the database and associated management functions from the application programs. Thus, changes in the database do not affect the application programs and vice versa.
3. **Data retrieval, analysis, modification and storage:** These are the basic functions of a DBMS. These are incorporated in the interface or command language provided for the application programs. The design objective here is to provide the functionality in such a way as to minimise the amount of coding in individual applications.
4. **Password:** DBMSs provide facilities which restrict the retrieval and modification of data by unauthorised users. This is usually achieved by using passwords associated with different types of data, files, and individual records and operations.
5. **Integrity control and recovery methods:** Integrity control involves the enforcement of certain rules governing the data and provision of some form of automatic 'audit trial' as insurance against possible system failure.[10] Recovery systems are provided to allow application(s) to be restarted after a system failure and will playback the transactions which occurred before the failure.
6. **Compatibility:** Compatibility denotes the ability of a DBMS to function in concert with the desired machine environment, programming languages and data as initially available.
7. **Concurrency support:** Concurrency support is the

ability of the DBMS to manage the kind of multi-user access problems which may arise when more then one user use the system simultaneously.

8. Support of complex file structures and access paths: The spectrum of functions in large application environment should be supported by the DBMS with reasonable efficiency to achieve the cost and performance goals of the applications.

3.6 FILE MANAGEMENT SYSTEM (FMS)

A computer operates on data which may be read from input from a terminal, generated by a program, or stored on an external storage device. Large volumes of data are commonly stored in external memory as objects called files[3]. File management systems were introduced to give programmers a consistent set of routines for managing files of computer-stored records.

File management means different things to different people. An application programmer sees file management as dealing with the structuring of data so that the various operations, *viz.*, sorting and searching of files, addition and deletion of records from files, *etc.*, can be executed efficiently. To a systems programmer, a file management system is one that

— allocates and manages buffers;
— creates and maintains directories for locating files;
— accesses records;
— creates and updates tables in internal memory that indicate the status of files being used by a programmer; and
— allocates/deallocates, and maintains storage space on secondary storage devices.

File management systems provide the ability to create records in a file, according to a particular specification, to add, modify and delete records, and sort them into specific orders before printing them in a variety of formats[1].

Consider a simple library system consisting of three applications, one each for

— issue of books;
— reservation of books; and
— recall of overdue books.

Suppose we have four files:

— the book file consisting details of library books;
— the loan file consisting details of the books already lent to borrowers;
— the borrower file consisting details of the borrowers; and
— the reservation file consisting details of the books reserved by the borrowers.

Figure 3.1 illustrates a simple file approach to the sample library system. It may be noted from Figure 3.1 that the 'Loan Program' consults three files, namely, the 'Loan File', the 'Borrower File', and the 'Book File'. Similarly, the 'Reservation Program' consults three files, namely, the 'Reservation File' the 'Book File', and the 'Loan File'. The 'Overdue Program' consults two files—the 'Loan File' and the 'Borrower File'. Problems of this approach are discussed in the following section.

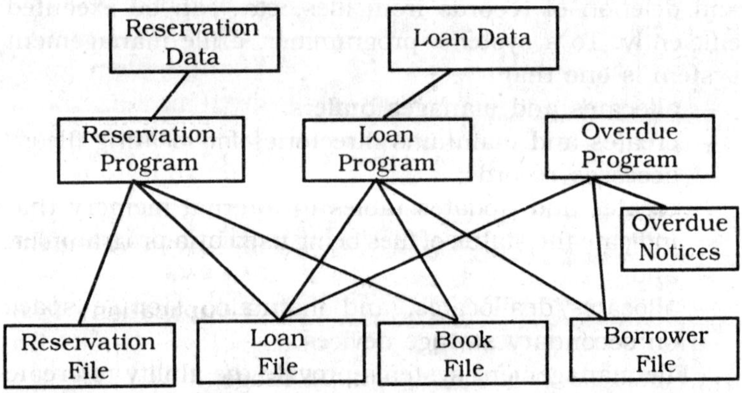

Figure. 3.1: File Approach to Sample Library System

3.7 DBMS *Vs.* FMS

Both FMSs and DBMSs utilise access methods to handle the details of physical access to/from storage devices. An access method is a layer of software whose function is to cancel all device-dependent details from the FMS and DBMS. Since DBMSs are normally built on top of an operating system, they may use the same access methods as the operating system's FMS[3].

Although, broadly speaking, DBMSs is a kind of File Management System (FMS), there is a fine distinction between the two. While FMSs are meant for physical arrangement of data, DBMSs are designed to deal with the logical arrangement of data. A further distinction relates to the capabilities of both the systems. The difference lies in the ability of the DBMS to handle highly-structured data. This is possible because in a DBMS the relationships among different data elements are reflected in what is called a 'conceptual schema'. Secondly, very high level language facilities are provided in a DBMS for retrieving and manipulating the data. Such facilities are not available in FMS.

The DBMS approach affords a solution to the problems of data independence and sharing of data across application programs that are encountered with FMSs. Problems of data inconsistency and data redundancy are greatly reduced in DBMS due to the provision of centralised mechanism for control of all data in the database. To be specific, a DBMS has the following properties which distinguish it from a file management system[3]:

— It is integrated with different applications using the same database;
— it reduces the possibilities of data duplication;
— it enhances data independence;
— it makes provision for shared usage;
— it permits finer granularity; and
— it permits control of security.

According to Oxborrow[5], the traditional file approach may

be seen as a program-oriented approach, while the database approach is essentially data-oriented. In traditional file management systems, some files are shared by different programs and each program uses a number of apparently independent files. Thus, it is the application program which has to keep track of the files which are relevant.

In a database approach, the database will be physically stored in a set of files but users and applications do not need to know anything about the physical storage. A description of the database will be stored along with the actual data; the description is like a complex directory which enables the database management system to retrieve data from the database and to store new data in the appropriate place in the database, establishing relationship with the other data, if relevant.[5]

Thus, the difference between the traditional file approach and database approach has resulted in a change in the emphasis on the systems analysis and design stages of information systems development. More attention is now paid towards data modelling and database design. In summary, database management systems aim at solving a number of specific problems (summarised in Table 3.1) which are associated with traditional file management systems.

3.8 COMPONENTS OF A DBMS

Three major components of a DBMS are: data definition language, data manipulation language, and query and reporting systems.

3.8.1 Data Definition Language

Data definition language is the vehicle through which the database designer specifies the rules that govern the data to be stored and retrieved. This allows specification of the types and formats of the fields. It also allows the designer to describe how individual items relate to each other.

Table 3.1: FMSs *Vs.* DBMSs

FMSs	*DBMSs*
1. Difficult to model the real world	Data structuring facilities enable to represent real world objects and their relationships
2. Low responsive to changes	Effects of changes are minimised due to data independence
3. High development costs due to specific application-oriented programs	Applications can be built easily with high-level data manipulation languages
4. Difficult to get answers to adhoc queries	Simple query languages are available (*e.g.*, QBE)
5. Low data reliability, security, and integrity due to decentralised nature of data	Centralised control of reliability, security, and integrity are available

3.8.2 Data Manipulation Language

Data manipulation language provides the operations which are required by the application programs. These operations are:

- — creation of records;
- — disconnecting the records;
- — finding records;
- — modifying data;
- — locking records in a multi-user environment;
- — connecting records;
- — deleting records;
- — retrieving data; and
- — initialising recovery.

3.8.3 Query and Reporting Systems

Query languages and facilities depend on the nature of interface provided by the system. The Query By Example (QBE) approach of IBM's SQL is example of systems which try to get away from forcing query statements to follow rigid system or to imply knowledge of the database structure.[3]

Reporting facilities provided by DBMSs involve creation of desired format for display and printing of the search results.

3.9 DATABASE DEVELOPMENT

Database development involves the construction of an actual database and it involves five major activities, *viz.*,

1. data investigation;
2. data modelling;
3. database design;
4. database implementation; and
5. database monitoring and tuning.

Table 3.2 represents the different processes, the underlying tasks, and the end results.

Table 3.2: Steps in Database Development

Process	*Tasks involved*	*End results*
Data investigation	Identification of nature and use of data	Data Dictionary
Data modelling	Shaping real world facts into real world concepts	Generalised conceptual model
Database design	Mapping conceptual model into DBMS—specific data model	DBMS-specific conceptual schema and external schema
Database implement-tation	Structuring the actual data in the physical data-base	Internal schema and database
Database monitoring and tuning	Monitoring database usage and restructuring database, if required	Optimised database

3.9.1 Data Investigation

Data investigation involves identification of the nature and use of data in an organisation. Information to be collected would include details of the

— objects in the system;
— constraints on the objects;
— relationships between objects;
— physical characteristics of objects, *etc.*

Oxborrow[5] divides the facts into three main categories, *viz.*, basic facts, constraints, and rules. In case of a library database, the following facts would be amongst those that are relevant:

Basic facts

- — a book has a title, author, publisher, publication year, class number, *etc.*
- — a book possesses a unique ISBN;
- — a book possesses a unique accession number when it is taken into the stock of a library;

Constraints

- — the ISBN consists of 13 characters of the following format:
  n-nnn-nnnnn-X or n-nnnnn-nnn-X (where n stands for a decimal and X stands for a decimal digit or the character 'X').
- — a book may be borrowed for different period of time by different category of users. For example, students may be able to borrow an item for a week, say, a researcher may be able to borrow for two weeks, a teacher may be able to borrow for four weeks, and so on.
- — limit on the number of items those can be borrowed may vary from user to user. For example, loan limit for students may be five, say, while that for researchers and teachers may be ten and fifteen respectively, and so on.

Rules

- — if the date due for return (for a book) is less than the current date then the book is overdue.
- — if the date of expiry (of membership) is less than the current date then the membership is expired.

In addition, the data investigation stage also reveals functional information about the use of data, like what types of functions will be carried out on the data, for example, in a library database a book may be issued, returned, renewed, reserved, and so on. The facts collected at the data investigation stage and expanded/refined later on should be organised and stored in a way suitable for easy reference by database designers and administrators, system developers, and the end-users. The end-product of such an organisation is the *data dictionary*.

3.9.2 Data Modelling

This step involves shaping of the facts, collected during the data investigation process, into data model concepts, and thereby deriving a conceptual model. The basic facts, the rules, constraints and the functional information are all important at this stage. The conceptual model is required to support present applications as well as future requirements. The model thus should not only reflect the present view but should also reflect future directions.

3.9.3 Database Design

Each database management system has its own specific rules, constraints, and limitations which apply to the data model. The process of database design is that of mapping the generalised data model into the specific data model of the given database management system. The conceptual schema, derived at this stage, is thus the description of the database written in the data description language provided by the database management system.

3.9.4 Database Implementation

At this stage the internal or storage schema is created by reference to the DBMS data model and other information obtained during the data investigation stage. Decisions are made regarding the physical database characteristics, *viz.*, file organisation, access methods, *etc.*, and the actual database is created.

3.9.5 Database Monitoring and Tuning

When the database is in operation, its usage is monitored to detect any errors, inefficiencies, omissions, *etc.* The monitoring process may call for certain restructuring of the existing database. Thus, this process helps to improve the database system as a whole. Database development is a continuous process.

3.10 DBMS—ARCHITECTURE

There are three kinds of database management systems. They are identified by the way data is organised (and accessed) in them. The three design approaches are:

hierarchical, network, and relational; these are widely discussed in literature[10-13]. The following sections briefly describe the nature and features of these database models.

3.10.1 Hierarchical Model

In a hierarchical structure, the data in records is organised into a hierarchy of fields and sub fields. A hierarchy is an inverted tree type of structure, with a single root object at the top and branch objects hanging from the root. At each branch level, a particular object may only be connected to one object at a higher level. The advantages of this structure include the simplicity of the individual pointers and the relatively efficient access afforded to the individual elements. Maintenance and change of this type of structure are straightforward and can be carried out by someone other than the original database designer[10]. Hierarchical structures do not, however, enable the programs (and consequently the users) to go from one particular field in a given record to the same field in the next record. To do this it is necessary to go at the top of the hierarchy and thereby slowing down the process.[7]

When a tree structure is available to represent the relationships between record types in a natural way, hierarchical database system affords an efficient implementation of the search and retrieval problem. However, hierarchies appear to be restrictive in many situations. Suppose, in an industrial environment, each manager handles many projects and many employees, and some employees are assigned to many projects. Under such circumstances, if we want to represent a hierarchical representation of the database, a great deal of stored information must have to be duplicated and jumps are necessary from one tree to another to access to the appropriate portions of the database. This happens because the first assumption, *i.e.*, each manager handles more than one project and many employees, requires that both the EMPLOYEE and PROJECT nodes will be subordinate to the MANAGER node. The project node will have information like project name, project number, *etc.*, associated with it, while the EMPLOYEE node will have employee details like employee name, address, age, salary, and so on. Now, because of the second assumption, *i.e.*, some employees are assigned to many projects, a many-to-one relationship exists between projects and managers, and between projects and employees. Such a structure is not allowed in a hierarchy because the PROJECT records now have two hierarchically superior record types.

The problem, mentioned above, can be solved by introducing logical pointers which introduce non-hierarchical relationships into the database system without abandoning the basic hierarchical structure. Figure 3.2 illustrates the resulting hierarchy.

It may be noted that normal hierarchical arrangement accommodates only many-to-one and one-to-one relationships. However, many-to-many relationships occur in many situations. A direct way for implementing many-to-many relationships between two record types consists in creating a third record type representing the intersection between the two original types of records.[9] The many-to-many relationships can then be represented by the conventional many-to-one pointers between each of the original record types and the newly defined intersection records. Suppose, in the example under discussion, the intersection records could specify the percentage of time each employee spends on a particular project. Figure 3.3 illustrates the use of intersection records.

The use of logical and physical pointers and intersection record types adapts the hierarchical database model to most processing requirements. Each record is stored with its descendants in succession. Access to the structure can be obtained at the *root*, *i.e.*, at the top of the tree structure diagram. An index is provided to access the record constituting the root. To find a particular record in the tree, the index is consulted to find a particular record among the

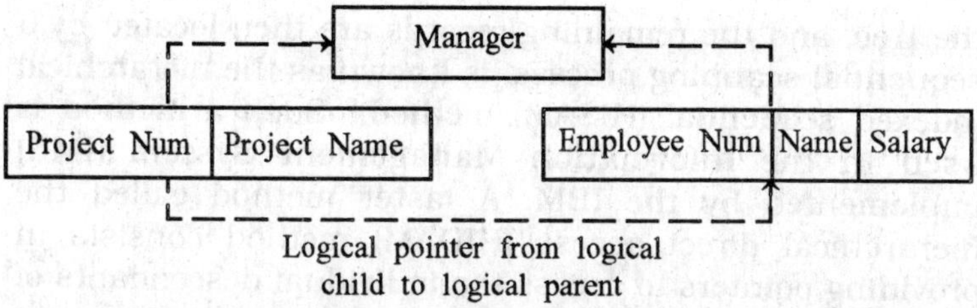

Figure. 3.2: Hierarchical Database structure showing Logical Pointers

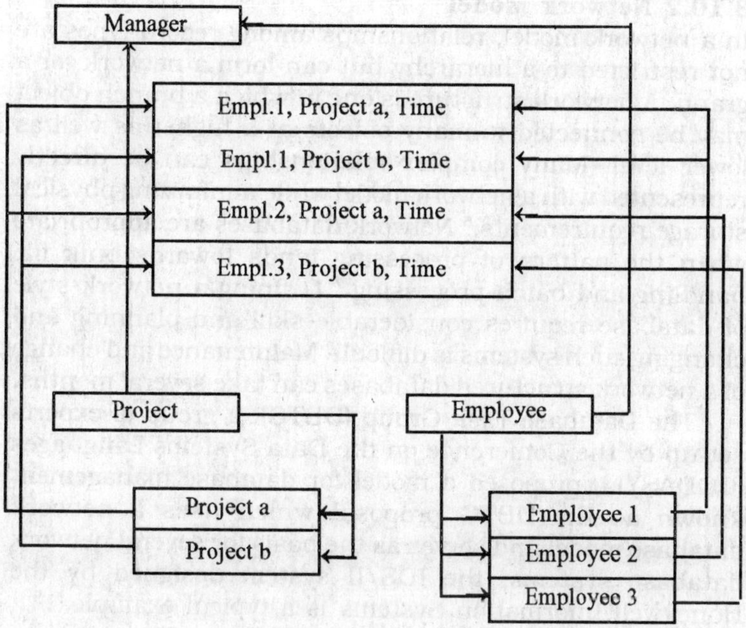

Figure. 3.3: Hierarchical Database Structure showing Intersection Records

root records, and then the pointers are followed to reach the corresponding child records. The list is then scanned until the wanted record is located. In order to accommodate new child records, an overflow storage area is used. Records that do not fit into the primary area are pushed to the overflow area. Such an arrangement where immediate access are obtained only to certain records at the root of the tree, and the remaining records are then located by a sequential scanning process, is known as the hierarchical indexed sequential (HISAM) method.[9] Such a method is used in the Information Management System (IMS) implemented by the IBM. A faster method called the hierarchical direct access (HIDAM) method consists in providing pointers to access the individual descendants of each root record.

3.10.2 Network Model

In a network model, relationships among record types are not restricted to a hierarchy but can form a network, or a graph. A network structure is one in which a branch object may be connected to many objects at a higher as well as lower level. Many complex relationships can be directly represented with a network model while minimizing physical storage requirements.[5] Network databases are appropriate when the pattern of processing tends towards bulk file handling and batch-processing.[7] Defining a network-style of database requires considerable skill and planning and changing such systems is difficult. Maintenance and change of a network structured databases can take several months.

The Database Task Group (DBTG), a group of experts set up by the Conference on the Data Systems Languages (CODASYL), proposed a model for database management known as the DBTG proposal which uses a network database model and serves as the basis for several network database systems; the IDS/II system designed by the Honeywell Information Systems is a typical example.[5, 9]

In a network model, several different many-to-one relationships can be defined from a single record type. The greater complexity of the relationships in the network model simplifies the navigation in the database, but the file access becomes more complicated. Figure 3.4 illustrates a network database implementation which presupposes that a given book supplier may supply books to many libraries, and a given library may have many suppliers. Suppose, we have three different kinds of records, *viz.*, Library, Supplier, and Book. Again, two new record types can be introduced, the first one labelled "Quantity" which provides the number of books ordered by a particular library, and the second one known as "Price" which states the price of a given book supplied by a supplier.

It may be noted from Figure 3.4 that the pointer chains can be followed from any particular record to any other related record, though the structure is somewhat complex. Errors in a search are avoided by using the currency pointers which identify the last record of each record type that was accessed at each particular point, as well as the last accessed record in each database set.

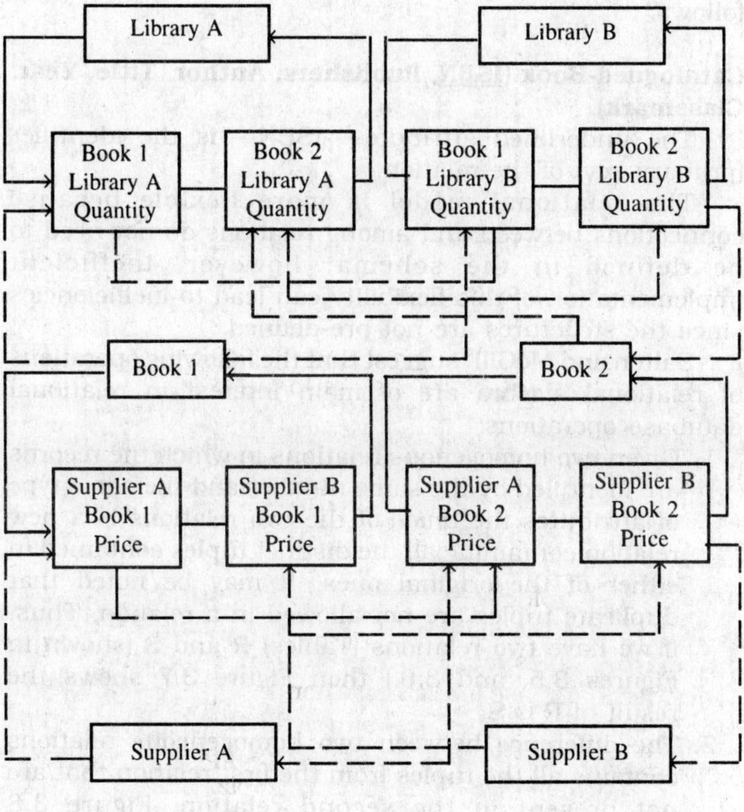

Figure. 3.4.: Network Database Implementation

3.10.3 Relational Model

The relational approach to data modelling was introduced by E.F. Codd in the late sixties.[14] It is based on the mathematical concepts of relations and sets. A relation represents an entity set or some aspects of an entity set, and the attributes of a relation are attributes associated with the entity set which it represents. Thus, the relational model is an entity-based model. A relation is a set of *tuples*. Relations are frequently represented as tables, in which rows represent tuples and columns represent *attributes*. A relation may be described by its name and its associated attributes; a simple description of the relation representing the catalogued book entity from the library model is as follows:

Catalogued-Book (<u>ISBN</u>, Publishers, Author, Title, Year, Classmark).

The underlined attribute----ISBN----is the identifier (primary key) of the relation.

The relational model is more flexible because connections between and among relations do not need to be defined in the schema; however, inefficient implementation of this flexibility can lead to inefficiencies since the structures are not pre-defined.[2]

Salton and McGill[9] suggest that the following operations of relational algebra are of main interest in relational database operations:

1. Given two homogenous relations in which the records are identified by the same number and the same type of attributes the *union* of the two relations is a new relation containing all the distinct tuples contained in either of the original ones. It may be noted that duplicate tuples are not allowed in a relation. Thus, if we have two relations (Tables) R and S (shown in Figures 3.5. and 3.6.) then Figure 3.7 shows the result of $R \cup S$.
2. The difference between two homogeneous relations contains all the tuples from the first relation that are not present in the second relation. Figure 3.8

represents the R—S relation (Figures 3.5 and 3.6 represent R and S relations respectively).

Name	Age	City
Chowdhury	34	Calcutta
Chowdhury	40	Calcutta
Chatterjee	50	Calcutta

Figure 3.5 Relation R

Name	Age	City
Chowdhury	40	Calcutta
Sen	50	Calcutta

Figure 3.6: Relation S

Name	Age	City
Chowdhury	34	Calcutta
Chowdhury	40	Calcutta
Chatterjee	50	Calcutta
Sen	50	Calcutta

Figure 3.7 R ∪ S Relation

Name	Age	City
Chowdhury	34	Calcutta
Chatterjee	50	Calcutta

Figure 3.8 The R—S Relation

3. A *selection* operation can be used to choose certain rows of a relation, depending on the condition(s) imposed on the values of certain attributes. The general notation used to choose certain tuples from the relation R is

   SELECT $_F$ (R) [where F is the formula expressing a condition]

Thus the expression

SELECT $_{(\text{Name = Chowdhury})}$ (R)

will show all records in R whose Name attribute is "Chowdhury" (see Figure 3.9).

Chowdhury	34	Calcutta
Chowdhury	40	Calcutta

Figure. 3.9: The SELECT Operation

4. *Projection* is the converse of select operation. In a projection certain columns from the original relation are chosen to form a new relation; duplicate nodes are, however, rejected. Thus the projection

   PROJECT $_{(3,\ 1)}$ (r)

   will produce a new relation as is shown in Figure 3.10. The new relation is created by taking column 3 followed by column 1 from the relation R (Figure 3.5). Project operations are useful to break down large complex relations into smaller and simple ones.

Calcutta	Chowdhury
Calcutta	Chatterjee

Figure. 3.10: The PROJECT Relation

5. The *Cartesian Product* (R × S) of two relations R and S is a new relation consisting of all possible unique tuples obtained by taking a tuple R followed by a tuple S. Thus, the length of the rows in R × S is equal to the sum of the length of tuples in R plus the length of tuples in S. The Cartesian Product operation can be used to construct a single large relation from two or more smaller relations. Figure 3.11 shows a Cartesian Product of the two relations R (Figure 3.5) and relation S (Figure 3.6).

Chowdhury	34	Calcutta	Chowdhury	40	Calcutta
Chowdhury	34	Calcutta	Sen	50	Calcutta
Chowdhury	40	Calcutta	Chowdhury	40	Calcutta
Chowdhury	40	Calcutta	Sen	50	Calcutta
Chatterjee	50	Calcutta	Chowdhury	40	Calcutta
Chatterjee	50	Calcutta	Sen	50	Calcutta

Figure. 3.11 The Cartesian Product Operation

The five basic operations described above can be used to generate additional useful operations. The *Join Operation*, which is a special kind of Cartesian Product operation, is of particular interest. The Join Operation forms a single relation from two initially given relations based on certain conditions of equality and inequality among the attribute values included in the relations. Two types of Join Operators, namely, Natural (*i.e.*, unrestricted), and Unnatural (*i.e.*, restricted) are available.

In case of restricted join operation, conditions are imposed on the values of attributes from the original relation.

If the columns in the relations R and S (Figures 3.5 and 3.6) are numbered as A, B, C, and D, E, F, respectively, then the join operation

R JOIN $_{(B < E)}$ S

implies that the joined relation consists of the tuples which result by taking a tuple from relation R followed by a tuple in relation S, such that the value of attribute B in relation R be smaller than the value of attribute E in relation S. Figure 3.12 illustrates the result of such a restricted Join.

Chowdhury	34	Calcutta	Chowdhury	40	Calcutta
Chowdhury	34	Calcutta	Sen	50	Calcutta
Chowdhury	40	Calcutta	Sen	50	Culcutta

Figure 3.12: The Restricted Join Operation

The Unrestricted Join is similar to the Restricted Join except that the join condition is assumed to be the equality of the components for the columns representing identical attributes. Thus, the operation

R JOIN S is equivalent to the restricted join

R JOIN $_{(B = E)}$ S

Figure 3.13 illustrates the unrestricted join operation. Here each tuple is generated by superimposing one tuple from relation R on one from relation S provided they have the same value in columns B and E.

Chowdhury	40	Calcutta
Chatterjee	50	Calcutta

Figure. 3.13: The Unrestricted Join Operation

3.11 RELATIONAL DBMS (RDBMS)

Relational databases provide the advantages of rapid access to file components. Relational DBMSs are so called because the data that they can manipulate are 'stored' as relations; these relations are in the form of data tables in which the information is arranged in rows and columns.[10] In other words, as discussed earlier, a file in relational system is considered to be a two-dimensional table known as a relation, where each record or tuple appears as row, while each column represents the assignment of values of some file attribute to the records of the collection.

The basic idea behind relational system is that the collection of data which is to constitute a database should be organised into groupings of different kinds, so that a particular kind of information will be given only once in one grouping, and nowhere else.[7]

One important concept in RDBMS is the functional dependency. An attribute Y is functionally dependent on another attribute X if the two tuples having the same value for X are required to also have the same value for Y.[2] These dependencies are used to determine normal forms for relations, in which the types of data and data dependencies that are allowed are restricted to avoid redundancies in storage of data.

When two relations contain at least one common attribute, they can be joined to form a combined relation, which is formed by juxtaposing all pairs of tuples from the individual relations for which the attribute values of the common attribute agree in each case. Tables 3.3, 3.4, 3.5 and 3.6 show examples of this. A large relation can be formed by joining these tables.

In the first two tables, the common key is the 'Publisher name'. As these two Tables are related, information can be retrieved by combining data from Tables 3.3 and 3.4, *e.g.*, 'name of the journal published by a given publisher, say, Pergamon Press'. Similarly, Tables 3.5 and 3.6 are related by the key 'Author name'; and Tables 3.4 and 3.6 are related by the key 'Journal name'. Now if we want to know the details of a work by a given author, we can easily do so, because by virtue of the relation between Tables 3.5 and 3.6, we get the article of the given author, its source journal, and year of publication. Again as Tables 3.4 and 3.6 are related, we get the information relating to the publisher and editor of the source journal. Finally, by virtue of the relation between Tables 3.3 and 3.4 we may know the address of the publisher. Hence, we get the full information required, by giving just one search key. For example, by searching through the author key we can learn that 'A.F. Smeaton of Dublin University has a publication on Natural Language Processing in the journal Information Processing & Management in the year 1990'.

Thus, the main advantage of a relational DBMS is its ability to access more than one file at a time, provided that the files in question have at least one field in common. The data manipulation languages in relational databases are, however, complex ones.

Relational databases also provide facilities for continuous updating. They also facilitate data security and it is comparatively easy to have in the system information about individual relations that determines which categories of users may have access to the data contained in them.[7] However, there are certain criticisms of relational DBMS. Kemp[7] mentions three major criticisms, *viz.*

1. The concept of RDBMS came up to satisfy the need to optimise the use of hardware available in early seventies; the common pattern was to have a large central processor, of that time, with (unsophisticated) terminals attached to it. Some aspects of relationality are less significant to the modern systems with the capacity of distributed processing.
2. Some people argue that relational database management systems are based on such mathematical foundations which do not completely describe relations.
3. Some people also argue that there are no real reasons why a database should not have repeating and variable length fields while retaining the other advantages of being relational.

Table 3.3: Publisher Information

Publisher Name	*Publisher Address*
Pergamon Press	New York
Elsevier	Amsterdam

Table 3.4: Journal Information

Journal Name	*Publisher Name*	*Journal Editor*
Inf. Proc. & Man.	Pergamon Press	Tefko Saracevic
Jour. of Inf. Sc.	Elsevier	Alan Gilchrist
....	....	....

Table 3.5: Author Information

Author Name	*Author Address*
A.F. Smeaton	Dublin University, Ireland
T. Saito	Hokkaido University, Japan

Table 3.6: Article Information

Title	*Author Name*	*Journal Name*	*Year*
Natural language processing	A.F. Smeaton	Inf. Proc. & Man.	1990
A clustering method	T. Saito	Jour. of Inf. Sc.	1990
....	....	....	....

3.11.1 Benefits of RDBMS

The basic advantages of relational database systems can be summarised as follows.[10]

1. **Easily visualised:** Some fairly complex relationships in the tree or network structures can easily be represented in relational model.
2. **Precision:** While a network representation can be quite complex and thus confusing, relationships expressed as joined tables are precise in meaning and quickly reveal inconsistencies in the database content or design.
3. **Security:** Sensitive data items can be isolated into separate relations and tagged with password for security.
4. **Reliability:** Relational model provides much more reliability on data.
5. **Ease of implementation:** The physical storage of relational tables are less complex than the storage of network or hierarchical structures.
6. **Data independence:** In relational model the database can grow without, in most cases, forcing the

rewriting of application programs.

7. **Data manipulation language:** With the data organized in the form of tables, the manipulation sub-language can be simple to use and extremely powerful in its way of operations.

3.11.2 Interacting with RDBMSs—the SQL

SQL (Structured Query Language) has emerged as the standard data language for accessing relational databases. Prior to SQL, there was no standard data access language. The SQL relational database interface was developed by the IBM in the late seventies. Implemented by IBM in their main database product (DB2) in 1982, SQL was adopted by the American National Standards Institute (ANSI) as the standard data access language in 1986. The ISO (International Standards Organisation) has also adopted SQL as the standard language for relational database management system access.

Applications written in the SQL can be moved from one computer platform to another. Software vendors have added their own extensions to the SQL which fill gaps in the Language. ORACLE has followed the ANSI standard, and they have also provided SQL*Plus extensions to the standard language.[15]

SQL consists of common English words such as SELECT, CREATE, *etc.*, which one can arrange in highly structured commands and statements in order to access and manipulate data stored in a relational database. The standard set of SQL commands falls into four categories, namely.

1. Data Definition Language (DDL) commands which are for creating and altering the structure of the database.
2. Data Manipulation Language (DML) commands which are for adding and modifying data.
3. Data Control Language (DCL) commands which are for controlling access to the database.
4. Query commands which are used to extract information from the database. Following are some of the common SQL commands:

Command	*Description*
ALTER PARTITION	Adds a file to a database partition
ALTER SPACE	Alters a space definition
ALTER TABLE	Adds a column to, or redefines a column in, an existing table
AUDIT	Audits use of a table, view, synonym, or system facility
COMMENT	Inserts into the data dictionary a comment about a table or a column
CREATE CLUSTER	Creates a cluster which may contain two or more tables
CREATE DATABASE LINK	Creates a link to a user name in a remote database
CREATE INDEX	Create an index for a table
CREATE PARTITION	Creates a new partition in the database
CREATE SPACE	Creates a space definition which then may be used to define the space allocation properties of a table
CREATE SYNONYM	Creates a synonym for a table or view name
CREATE TABLE	Creates a table and defines its column and other properties
CREATE VIEW	Defines a view of one or more tables or other views
DELETE	Deletes one or more row from a table or view
DROP	Deletes a cluster, database link, index, space definition, synonym, table, or a view from the database
GRANT	Grants system and object database privileges to the user
INSERT	Adds new rows to a table or view
LOCK TABLE	Permits shared access to the table by multiple users while preserving the table's integrity
NOAUDIT	Partially or completely reverses the effect of a prior AUDIT command or of auditing options in a default table

RENAME	Changes the name of a table, view or a synonym
REVOKE	Revokes database system or object access privileges from users
SELECT	Performs a query and selects rows and columns from one or more tables or views
UPDATE	Changes the values of fields in a table or view
VALIDATE INDEX	Checks the integrity of a table index

The basic construct in SQL is the SELECT-FORM-WHERE specification, where the select part specifies the attributes actually wanted, the FROM portion identifies the relation in which these attributes occur, and the WHERE clause introduces an expression characterizing the attribute values previously named[9]. Thus, the following formulation:

```
SELECT EMPLOYEE_NAME, EMPLOYEE_NUM
    FROM EMPLOYEES
    WHERE SALARY > = 2000
    AND DEPT = 2
```

produces names and numbers of all the employees from the EMPLOYEE table who work in DEPT number 2 and whose salary is at least 2000. Thus, a language such as SQL uses linguistic constructs for query specification.

3.11.3 QBE (Query By Example)

The well-known QBE is a commercial tabular querying system specifically adapted to the relational database model. QBE, which is a two-dimensional screen-oriented query language, initially provides the user with an empty table *skeleton* in a default format. The user then specifies a query by marking columns as desired, thereby eventually entering an 'example'. The columns in the table are filled in with appropriate instructions and values of attributes. Two kinds of values are distinguished in QBE, *viz.*

— values which are taken 'literally' where the value shown is directly used as an operand; and

— values which are used as samples to designate 'unknown values' of corresponding attributes.

Thus, the query presented in Table 3.7 will produce all the publications in the named journal (*i.e.*, Inf. Proc. & Man.). Here the journal name has been given as a literal (provided in double quotes).

Table 3.7: Sample Query-By-Example

Title	*Author Name*	*Journal Name*	*Year*
		"Inf. Proct & Man"	

3.12 DISTRIBUTED DATABASE SYSTEMS

A distributed database system is one where different databases are geographically dispersed and can be accessed and managed remotely via a network. Consider a large organisation with a corporate headquarter in one city and several regional headquarters in other cities across the nation. A distributed database system could have a central database facility at the corporate headquarter and smaller database system facilities at the regional headquarters. The regional installations could be used for localized database processing tasks such as payroll, inventory management, marketing activities, *etc.* These regional systems could be used as remote stations for interacting with the central corporate computer.

Technical support for a distributed database environment requires a capability to provide communications hardware and software that link the interacting parties (offices or employees). This network can be as simple as the connection provided implicitly when all workers are accessing the same system via video display terminals, or as complex as when different processors are linked together through a LAN (Local Area Network) or a WAN (Wide Area Network).

3.12.1 Advantages of Distributed Databases

There are many potential advantages of the distributed database approach in comparison to the centralised database approach. Some of these are:

1. Data entry tends to be greatly improved in a distributed environment because local sites tend to be more familiar with the data than the central corporate office. Obvious mistakes that might not be detected at a central location are recognised and corrected locally.
2. Small database processing tasks can be completed on the local equipment without incurring the communications costs involved in a strictly centralised environment.
3. Communication costs are further reduced if only summary information need to be transmitted to the central processing location rather than unprocessed, detailed data.
4. Response time may be faster at a local site. Distributed databases also reduce the work load on the central computing facility.

3.12.2 Disadvantages of Distributed Databases

However, there are certain potential disadvantages of distributed database systems, *viz.*

1. Economics of scale may be lost. Large computers tend to process information faster than smaller ones. Therefore, the local computers may take longer to accomplish the data processing at the local site. Increased costs on replicating hardware, software, and data may offset savings in communication costs.
2. Unnecessary duplication of design and programming activity may occur at the local sites.
3. Local managers may not have the expertise needed to manage the database system and its equipment.

3.13 OBJECT-ORIENTED DATABASE SYSTEMS

Researches in the area of programming languages have influenced database systems to a significant extent. There is an increased interest today in descriptive languages, which has led to the concepts of logic programming as well as object-oriented programming. In the field of object-oriented programming, some people are working on adding database functionality to those languages or language environments. Therefore, object-oriented database systems can be considered as the merging of efforts in two previously distinct fields. The main characteristics of an object-oriented system are:

— objects, messages, and methods;
— data abstraction and encapsulation, types, and classes;
— object identity;
— inheritance; and
— overloading and late binding.

Hence, a database system can be considered object-oriented if it shares these characteristics and in addition, provides general DBMS functionality, as mentioned earlier. Typical examples of object-oriented programming languages are C++, Small talk, Modula2, Simula, *etc.* The GemStone system, marketed by Servio Logic Development Corporation, is an example of an object-oriented database management system.

Traditional database systems, whether hierarchical, network or relational, deal with simple data types—typically facts like name, age, address, salary, and so on, which reflect their origin in paper records. Object-oriented databases are intended to manage the complex objects. Ideally depositing or withdrawing a complex object from such a database should be a simple matter of sending and receiving the standard message construct. As informally defined by Klauss Dittrich[16], an object-oriented database allows us to represent one miniworld (application domain) entity by exactly one object in the database, whereas traditional database systems only allow complex objects to be represented indirectly as an ordered collection of simple entities or as an atomic object that is merely referenced or filed elsewhere. Object-oriented systems can provide more efficient access than if objects were merely composed from and decomposed to the types handled by traditional databases. Object-oriented database systems are still in the stage of research although a few prototype systems have already appeared. Frameworks for different information retrieval systems have also been designed on the top of object-oriented systems. Harper and Walker[17] have designed a system called ECLAIR which can be used to construct information retrieval systems and applications. ECLAIR is implemented in C++ and uses an object-oriented DBMS (called ONTOS) for persistent data storage; the library provides data structures and operations necessary to allow the efficient indexing, storage and retrieval of data items based on their text content using automatic indexing and best-match retrieval techniques.

3.14 MULTIMEDIA DATABASE SYSTEMS

Computer-based multimedia database or information systems have become a popular research topic in recent years.[18] The different kinds of technologies needed to implement multimedia database systems are optical discs for mass storage, high bandwidth network for fast access, and sophisticated workstations for meaningful representation and necessary manipulation.

The different kinds of data handled by multimedia systems are facts like name of person, job title, author, *etc.*, statistical data like figures, tabular data, *etc.*, texts, sound, music, and images like line or graphical drawings, paintings, engineering drawings, *etc.*

Traditional database management systems are designed to handle facts only whereas multimedia systems have to manage data differing widely in structure and size—from a text comment of a few bytes to a digitised photograph that may be a half megabyte array.

3.14.1 Features of Multimedia Systems

A multimedia system is supposed to store everything that can be represented digitally like simple facts, statistical data, textual data, sound, graphics, and images.

Once everything is stored, the user must be able to retrieve the data. Retrieval falls into two categories:

Presentation: Retrieval by presentation commonly applies to composite data *e.g.*, 'Find all the images.'

Content: Retrieval by content is the process of retrieving information according to their semantic content. The simplest method of content retrieval is based on manually generated labels, *i.e.*, descriptors entered from the keyboard by an operator. The other extreme is automatic semantic analysis, *i.e.*, descriptors inferred by the system.

Multimedia systems require modern workstations with huge storage capacity, high speed architecture, high resolution screen and distributed system environment. The management of multimedia information is a multi-disciplinary task, not always tackled by a multi-disciplined team. Notably implementations of multimedia information systems can learn much from experts in image/voice analysis and knowledge representation as well as from designers of traditional databases. Apple UK's 'Interactive Multimedia' is a hybrid system of video discs, CD-ROMs and other peripherals controlled by a Macintosh running hypercard.[18]

3.15 INTELLIGENT DATABASE SYSTEMS

With the advancements in information technology and influences from AI and expert systems technologies, a new concept has come up which aims at incorporating knowledge about the domain and thus aims at handling knowledge rather than mere data. Such systems are called intelligent database systems or knowledge-based systems. The basic idea is to incorporate a set of rules into the system which will help to create some kind of knowledge base.

Knowledge-based systems can be used in different areas of library and information science, *viz*

— reference and referral, question-answering systems;
— end-user searching;
— OPAC, etc.

Examples of knowledge-based systems are Reuter's TIS (Topic Identification Systems), CANSEARCH, PLEXUS, SCISOR, RESEARCHER, TINA, etc. Chapter 11 discusses knowledge-based systems in detail.

REFERENCES

1. P.F. Burton and J.H. Petrie, *The Librarian's Guide to Microcomputers for Information Management*, Van Nostrand Reinhold, 1986.

2. C.M. Eastman, Database management systems. In: M.E. Williams, editor, Annual Review of Information Science and Technology, Vol. 20, New York, Knowledge Industry Publications, 1985, pp. 91-115.
3. B.G. Claybrook, *File Management Techniques*, New York, John Wiley, 1983.
4. J.R. Rumble, Data, Computers, and Database Management Systems, In: Database Management in Science and Technology, ed. by J.R. Rumble and V.E. Hampel, Amsterdam, Elsevier Science Publishers, 1984, pp. 1-13.
5. E. Oxborrow, *Database and database management systems: concepts and issues*, Ed. 2. Chichester, Chartwell-Bratt, 1989.
6. G. Salton, *Automatic text processing: the transformation, analysis, and retrieval of information by computer*, Reading, MA, Addison-Wesley, 1989.
7. D.A. Kemp, *Computer-based knowledge retrieval*, London, Aslib, 1988.
8. J. Ashford, Storage and retrieval of bibliographic records: a comparison of database management system (DBMS) and free text approaches, *Program*, Vol. 18 No. 1, 1984, 16-45.
9. G. Salton and M.J. McGill, *Introduction to modern information retrieval*, New York, McGraw-Hill Book Co., 1983.
10. L.A. Kurtz, An introduction to database management systems, *Program*, Vol. 18, 1984, 1-15.
11. M. Collier, *Microcomputer Software for Information Management*, Aldershot, Gower, 1986.
12. Gottfried Vossen, *Data Models, database languages and database management systems*, Wokingham, England, Addison-Wesley Pub. Co., 1991.
13. J.F. Courtney and D.B. Paradice, *Database systems for management*, St. Louis, Times Mirror, 1988.
14. E.F. Codd, A Relational Model of Data for Large Shared Databanks, *Communications of the ACM*, Vol. 13, No. 6, 1970, 377-87.
15. James T. Perry and Joseph G. Lateer, *Understanding ORACLE*, New Delhi BPB Publications, 1989.
16. K.R. Dittrich, ed. Advances in object-oriented database systems. Proceedings of the 2nd International Workshop on object-oriented database systems. Berlin, Springer-Verlag, 1988.
17. D.J. Harper and A.M. Walker, ECLAIR: an extensive class library for information retrieval. *The Computer Journal*, Vol. 35, No. 3, 1992, 256-267.

18. M.H. O'Docherty and C.sN. Daskaiakis. Multimedia Information Systems—the Management and Semantic Retrieval of all Electronic Data Types. *The Computer Journal*, Vol. 34, No. 3, 1991, 225-238.

Chapter 4
Text Retrieval Systems

4.1 INTRODUCTION

The aim of an information retrieval system is to organise and store large amounts of text so that information can be retrieved from the repositories in response to users' information requests. Conventional information retrieval systems are based on assigning index terms to the stored documents which are subsequently used as keys for retrieval. These index terms are usually taken from the title of the concerned document or from the *subject statement.* Such subject statements are produced by human indexer on the basis of an analysis and interpretation of the whole text. This process involves too much abstraction of the information produced by the author in the given document and thus restricts the possibility of proper communication to the potential users. The process of human indexing is slow and demands much intellectual involvement.

Owing to the increasing number of documents produced in each subject field, it is becoming an uphill task for human indexers to manage the situation manually. Computerised information or text retrieval systems were developed to meet the growing demands of providing right information to the right user at the right time. Text retrieval systems allow users to conduct better search on the collection of texts. In fact, users can search through any term occurring in the title, abstract or even in the full text. Text retrieval systems thus not only perform the task of retrieval in a better way, but they also avoid the possibilities of loss of information caused by abstraction during the process of human indexing.

4.2 TEXT RETRIEVAL

Text retrieval systems are often referred to as textual information management systems (TIMS) in literature.[1]

These systems deal with various kinds of documents which are textual in nature. Conventionally, text retrieval systems deal with bibliographic documents/materials characterised by various keys like author, title, keywords, publication details, abstract, *etc.* Such systems enable users to search the bibliographic records through any of the keys like author name, title, assigned keywords, or by one or more words occurring in the abstract field. In such a situation, the text retrieval system acts as a bibliographic or reference retrieval system because the search retrieves one or more bibliographic records, and the users have to consult the hard copies of the documents to get the required information. This is the most conventional use of text retrieval systems in libraries. A number of software packages are available worldwide to serve this function.

However, text retrieval systems may also contain full texts of any kind of documents like letters, correspondences, office memos, legal documents, patient records and case histories, complete texts of articles and books, and so on. Users of such systems expect to retrieve the complete text or parts of it in response to a query and can go through it to get the desired information. Such systems, because they store the complete text of documents rather than mere bibliographic information of the same, take much disk space and the retrieval mechanism needs to be sophisticated to provide fast access to the records. These text retrieval systems are known as full text or free text retrieval systems, often designated as FTXs. The word free text often means that the text words are not pre-indexed and a separate index file is not maintained as is normally done in text retrieval systems, and therefore disk space for the large index file is saved. FTXs store the entire text of a document in ASCII or EBCDIC character form, and consequently those documents which are produced (or are available) in machine-readable form are suitable for storing in FTXs. This book discusses text retrieval systems as such without laying specific emphasis on full text retrieval systems *per se*.

Rowley[1] mentions that in text retrieval systems, the focus is on the storage and retrieval of text, rather than numeric, tabular or graphical data. However, complete texts often contain numeric and tabular data, but mostly it is textual. Text retrieval systems are designed to provide different access points to a database. A functional definition of a text retrieval system may be: a system that accepts, collates and stores textual information from a variety of sources, retrieves specific information from the text in response to queries, and processes the retrieved text in a user defined format.

Tetsky[2] mentions that an ideal text retrieval system must support three major functions, namely

— It should be able to deal with all kinds of documents collected from a variety of sources;

— It should organise and store all the documents in accordance with the pre-determined nature of the retrieval system; and

— It should have the capability to search the stored information in a user defined search criteria, and should allow users to edit the search results.

4.3 HISTORY OF TEXT RETRIEVAL SYSTEMS

The first text storage and implementation designed for a broad audience date back to the early seventies when on-line search services, such as DIALOG and ORBIT, introduced full text retrieval systems which indexed every word in the stored records[3].

Such implementations were initially short bibliographic records, some of which contained abstracts; Mead Data Central's LEXIS system was the first search service to produce online access to the complete text of documents.[4] Mead Data subsequently introduced the NEXIS system which provides online access to the complete text of newspapers, magazines, and other news-oriented publications. The number of text databases offered by on-line search services has increased significantly since the seventies. The *Directory of Online Databases*[5] enlists more than 4,000 on line databases.

Developed in the late sixties, IBM's STAIRS (Storage and Information Retrieval System) is, perhaps, the most widely implemented text storage and retrieval program for mainframe computers. Like STAIRS, the Battele Automated Search Information System (BASIS) and Infodata Corporation's INQUIRE system were developed in the late sixties and attracted many customers. Originally developed for IBM mainframe, BASIS is now available for a variety of mainframe and microcomputer environments.

BRS/Search, a STAIRS-derivative text storage and retrieval system developed for the BRS search service, has been available for in-house implementations since the late seventies. The DOCU/MASTER program, introduced for IBM mainframes by TSO International in the seventies, is now being marketed by Document Systems Inc. Several European text retrieval systems have been successfully implemented in a variety of government, commercial, and institutional applications. Three of the best known examples, *viz.*, ASSASIN, CAIRS, and STATUS, have been developed in the UK.

The number of mainframe and minicomputer text retrieval systems has increased steadily since the seventies. Introduced in the early eighties, microcomputer-based text retrieval systems, including products created specifically for microcomputers as well as implementations of programs originally developed for larger hardware configurations, have grown quite steadily.

Regular reviews of text retrieval packages appear in many publications. Saffady[4] presents a review of 34 packages; Dyer and Gunson[6] compile a directory of around 500 packages originating from 379 suppliers worldwide; and the IIS directory[7] reviews 100 software packages.

4.4 CHARACTERISTICS OF TEXT RETRIEVAL SYSTEMS

In general, a text retrieval software is characterised by the following features.[7]

- Variable length fields;
- Access to records through an inverted file of text terms which are drawn from the records of the database;
- A range of retrieval facilities which support retrieval based on words in records;
- Emphasis on the management of one or more distinct

databases; and

— Fixed applications which require limited or no knowledge of programming.

Handling free or full text calls for a specialised kind of software. The need for such a specialised software has to do with the nature of the free text itself. Text has some obvious attributes which make it difficult to process it in the same form as other kinds of data.[8] Full text systems may require specialised storage methods because sequences of text may range from a few hundred to millions of bytes.

For the purpose of storage, a text may be regarded as a very long string, whereas for the purpose of analysis, substrings of text may be identified and can be arranged in a hierarchic topology, for example, *document-section-paragraph-sentence-word*.[8] This model is adopted by most commonly available full text retrieval software.

Full text software systems are characterised by comprehensive indexing mechanisms so that large texts (say, over 10 Mbytes) can be rapidly searched for occurrences of particular strings.[8] If word-level indexing is used, an index associates each distinct word occurrence with its exact position in a document. Typical search criteria may include proximity matching, fuzzy or partial matching, and searching via an on line thesaurus.

4.5 FACILITIES OF TEXT RETRIEVAL SYSTEMS

Before going to select and implement a text retrieval software, it is essential to assess the potential benefits to be gained from such a software and to contrast the advantages with the costs. These costs will include cost of the software package and hardware, training and staff time.[9] However, benefits of a text retrieval system are not easy to quantify.

Major facilities offered by text retrieval software, and therefore available in a text retrieval system, can broadly be divided into four categories which are described in the following subsections.

4.5.1 Search Facilities

A text retrieval system is designed to provide various search facilities to its users. Facilities for query formulation with provisions for necessary search refinements with boolean operators, truncations, *etc.*, are expected from a text retrieval package. These issues are discussed later.

4.5.2 Help Facilities

Text retrieval systems are supposed to provide sufficient on line help facilities to the users.

4.5.3 Editing Database

Text retrieval systems are designed to provide adequate facilities to the users for editing the database. It also provides facilities for easy browsing of the database.

4.5.4 Formatting Search Results

Text retrieval systems provide facilities for editing and formatting the search results in a desired way.

4.6 FEATURES OF A TEXT RETRIEVAL SYSTEM

Basic features desirable for an ideal text retrieval system may broadly be categorised into two groups, *viz.*, database creation, and retrieval provisions. Features relating to each of these headings are discussed in the following sections.

4.6.1 Database Creation

Creation of database using a text retrieval package should be quite an easy task. This task is often performed by people with little computing skill, and thus the whole process of database creation should be quite simple. Text retrieval packages have certain basic features which are directly concerned with database creation performance and efficiency of the system. Following are some of the major features:

1. ***Variable length fields and records***

   In contrast to a traditional DBMS, where a given field occupies more or less the same length in each record, a text database is characterised by the fact that a given field in each record may not always be of the same length. For example, length of the abstract varies from record to record. Thus, prior allocation of fixed length for each field in a text database system may not be quite useful. Therefore, retrieval packages should accommodate variable length fields for best handling of the various text retrieval operations. Variable length fields help in making optimum use of storage space. Systems having fixed fields and records use disk space insufficiently because a number of blank spaces are left in a field.[10]

2. ***User-defined record structure***
   In text retrieval operations, it is always desirable that the structure of records in a given database be decided by the user (here, user denotes the database designer, not the end-user) according to his needs. In other words, user should be able to design the structure of the database to suit the specific needs. Most text retrieval systems provide this facility. In addition, user should also be able to decide which fields are to be indexed and which are not. This does not only save disk space, but also aids in retrieval operations.
3. ***Data entry and editing***
   Size of the database in a text retrieval system increases with the addition of new records. Most text retrieval packages provide facilities for online data entry and editing. However, entering records one by one in the database, particularly in case of retrospective data base creation, may be a tedious job. One solution to this could be to download the data from other source(s). This calls for entry of data in a batch mode. However, downloading data involves a number of considerations; the most important ones relate to the compatibility of formats and/or availability of a suitable program for conversion of data from one format to the other. Online editing of database is required at times, especially when the user wants to use the database for a specific purpose that was not envisaged to begin with.

4.6.2 Retrieval Provisions

Text retrieval software are characterisea by the availability of a wide variety of search and retrieval provisions. Features relating to retrieval provisions of a text retrieval package are described in the following paragraphs.

1. ***Boolean query formulation***

   A text retrieval system should provide for query formulation by using the boolean AND, OR, NOT operators and also provide nested boolean searching. Boolean search facilities allow a user to use more than one search term in a given search prescription with certain conditions imposed. These conditions specify whether more than one search term should simultaneously be present in the desired records, whether any one of some chosen words should be present, or one or more terms should be present while another term(s) should not be present in the desired records, and so on. Nested Boolean search facility allows to impose more complex conditions along with the search terms. The following search statements permitted in the BRS/Search software illustrate the use of Boolean operators.

   FISH AND CHIPS

   (will retrieve all records with the search terms FISH and CHIPS occurring in the same record)

   FISH OR CHIPS

   (will retrieve all those records where either of the search terms occur)

   FISH NOT CHIPS

   (will retrieve all those records where the search term FISH occurs and at the same time the term CHIPS does not occur)

   FISH XOR CHIPS

   (will retrieve all those records where either of the search terms occur but not both)

It may be noted that text retrieval software use different conventions for denoting the different Boolean operators. For example, in the STATUS software,

   FISH + CHIPS ?

   (will retrieve those records where both the search terms occur)

   FISH, CHIPS ?

   (will retrieve records containing either FISH or CHIPS)

Following is an example of nested Boolean search expression allowed in the CDS/ISIS software :

LIBRARY * (NETWORK + TELECOMMUNICATION)

will retrieve all those records where the terms LIBRARY and NETWORK occur, and also those records where the terms LIBRARY and TELECOMMUNICATION occur.

2. *Proximity searching*

In a text retrieval system, there should be a provision for adjacency/proximity searching. The purpose of this searching is to refine search statements by permitting the searcher to specify the context in which a term must occur. This search facility allows user to specify whether two search terms should occur adjacent to each other, whether one or more words occur in between the search terms, whether the search terms should occur in the same paragraph irrespective of the intervening words, and so on.

Following are some examples of proximity searches accepted in the BRS/Search software:

FISH SAME CHIPS

(will retrieve all records where the search terms, *i.e.*, FISH and CHIPS occur in the same paragraph)

FISH WITH CHIPS

(will retrieve all records where FISH and CHIPS occur in the same sentence)

FISH ADJ CHIPS

(will retrieve all records where FISH is followed by CHIPS in the same sentence)

FISH NEAR CHIPS

(will retrieve all those records where either FISH is followed by CHIPS or CHIPS is followed by FISH in the same sentence)

Text retrieval software differ in using notations for representing various proximity operators. Following are some examples of proximity searches allowed in CDS/ISIS.

MICROCOMPUTERS (G) LIBRARIES

(will retrieve all records where both the search terms occur in the same field)

INFORMATION • MANAGEMENT
or
INFORMATION $ MANAGEMENT

(will retrieve records where both the search terms occur and in between them at most one word may occur, *e.g.*, Information centre management, Information resources management, *etc.*)

3. *Search refinements*

The ability to specify a search strategy, and to elicit a response in terms of numbers of postings or records retrieved on the basis of that strategy is fundamental to most text retrieval system. This facility supports the narrowing or broadening of search strategies. Once a search statement is formulated, there should be provisions for refining it in a step-by-step fashion so as to arrive at an optimum level of retrieval.

4. *Range searching*

Range searching is most useful with numerical information. It is important in selecting records within certain data ranges. Following options are usually available for range searching:

— Greater than (>)
— Less than (<)
— Equal to (=)
— Not equals to (≠ or < >)
— Greater than equals to (>=)
— Less than equals to (<=)

These operators are used to prescribe a precise condition in a given search statement.

5. *Limiting searches*

The database in a text retrieval system comprises of different fields with different items of information. The user in his query formulation should be able to limit the search in one or more fields. Text retrieval software usually provide this facility. This is also known as field searching, whereby user can specify one or more fields where the search are to be looked for. Following are some examples:

from BRS/Search—

BIRD . PET

(will retrieve all records where the search term BIRD occurs in the paragraph (field) named PET)

from CDS/ISIS—

COMPUTERS * COMMUNICATIONS / (4)

(will retrieve those records where both the search terms occur in the field identified by the field tag 4).

6. *Display of postings*

A text retrieval system should display the number of postings for a given query in a given search. This helps user determine whether the number of items retrieved is more, less, or just right. Accordingly, he may just wish to view the retrieved records, print the retrieved records, or refine the search statement in order to arrive at a better result.

7. *Truncation*

Truncation is a search facility whereby a search can be conducted for all the different forms of a word having the same common root. As an example, the truncated word COMPUT* will retrieve items on COMPUTER, COMPUTING, COMPUTATION, COMPUTE, *etc.*

A number of different options are available for truncation, *viz.*, right truncation, left truncation, and masking of letters in the middle of the word. Left truncation retrieves all words having the same characters at the right hand part, *e.g.*, '*hyl' will retrieve words like 'methyl', 'ethyl', *etc.* Similarly, middle truncation retrieves all words having the same characters at the left and right hand part. For example, a middle truncated search term 'col*r' will retrieve both the terms 'colour' and 'color'. A 'wild card' is used to allow any letter to appear in a specific location within a word.

Following are some examples of truncated search allowed in BRS/Search:

FISH$

(will retrieve all records with words ending with FISH, *e.g.*, FISH, FISHES, FISHY, FISHING, *etc.*)

$FORM

(will retrieve all records with words ending with FORM, *e.g.*, INFORM, CONFORM, DEFORM, REFORM, *etc.*)

$FORM$

(will retrieve records with FORM embedded within, *e.g.*, INFORMATION, REFORMATION, DEFORMATION, CONFORMATION, *etc.*)

Nested Boolean searching is also possible with truncated search terms. Following is an example, from CDS/ISIS.

(INFORMATION * TECHNOLOG$) +
(COMPUTER$*COMMUNICATION$)

(will retrieve records on 'Information technology', 'Information technologies', *etc.*, as well as 'computer and communication', 'computers and communication', 'computers and communications', and so on).

8. ***String searching***

It is the ability to search on character strings within the body of the text in a record, which is usually available for those fields the text of which has not been included in an inverted file, and is, therefore, not pre-indexed. In other words, string searching allows one to search those terms which have not been indexed. However, as the process of string searching matches the search term character by character with the stored records, the search process is tremendously slow for a relatively large database.

Typically, text string searching may be used on a subset of the database, that subset having been retrieved by searching on indexed fields. Some text retrieval systems provide facility for string searching.

9. ***Stopword lists***

Use of stopword lists helps to avoid creation of inverted file for unsought words. A text retrieval system should make provisions for using stopword lists. This helps to reduce the size of the inverted file thereby making optimum use of the disk space and also making the search faster.

10. ***Index vocabulary control***

A text retrieval system should make provisions for

thesaurus support for helping users in choosing appropriate search terms. User can consult online thesaurus for choosing appropriate terms. If user is not satisfied with the output of a given search session, he may choose alternative search terms from the thesaurus.

11. ***Search term widening/narrowing***

Provision of a thesaurus can help users in widening or narrowing the search by using narrower, broader and related terms from the online thesaurus. This is particularly useful when the number of retrieved records in a given search session is too low or too high in accordance with the user's expectation.

12. ***Sorting of search results***

Sorted output from the retrieved results often are quite useful to the users. Users may want to sort all or a certain number of records in a database in a desired way. For example, users may want to sort the records in a bibliographic database by author, by title, and so on. Provisions for sorting results easily should be available from a text retrieval system.

13. ***Editing and formatting results***

Users of a text retrieval system may want to print all or a certain number of database records in a chosen format. For example, users of a bibliographic database may want to generate printed library catalogue, a bibliography, an index, and so on. Users may also want the output of a given search session in a typical format with necessary editing. Text retrieval systems should also make provision for printing of database records in a chosen format. Users should be able to view the database records in a suitable format, according to AACR2, say.

14. ***Data security***

In some cases, particular pieces of text, and sometimes the whole database need to be secured from unauthorised access to the database. In a library environment, end-users should be allowed to search the database without having a right to change the contents of the same. Thus, there should be a mechanism of securing the database from unauthorised access and alteration. Various kinds of securities are provided in text retrieval systems.

15. *Online help*

Users often need help in course of searching a database. Same is also required in course of database creation. Text retrieval systems should provide online help facilities available from any point of database creation or searching. Online, context-sensitive help make a text retrieval system more friendly to the users.

16. *Relevance feedback and ranked output*

This is an advanced retrieval feature where the system ranks documents or document segments by their presumed relevance and displays them in ranked sequence. It is particularly useful where a large database is searched and the number of retrieved items may also be large. The retrieval system asks relevance judgement from the user in course of search session and then these are used for ranking of retrieved items.

In addition to these basic features, many packages offer a variety of additional facilities which may assist in retrieval or even support specific applications. For example, CDS/ISIS has advanced programming facilities through which users can develop various application programs which are not readily available in the system.

Full text retrieval systems should be able to handle both bibliographic data as well as full texts of documents. In addition to providing keyword access, these software should discriminate word distances in order to facilitate proximity searching. Full text retrieval software must also recognise and facilitate the interactive nature of full text searching. Studies have shown that the average number of queries against a full text database prior to display can be ten or more.[3] Therefore, it is important that each result be located quickly and new criteria be added to refine the search process. Another useful feature is that which enables user to display retrieved records based on some heuristic determination of relevance to a search. Full text retrieval systems should highlight the search terms while displaying the retrieved records, and should allow document scrolling, preferably both backward and forward.

4.7 APPLICATIONS OF TEXT RETRIEVAL SYSTEMS

Many earlier information retrieval systems were, in fact, bibliographic retrieval systems, because the data those dealt with were bibliographic citations to documents, periodical articles, reports, conference proceedings, *etc.* The major objective of these databases were to locate references on a given topic or a particular document written by an author. True text retrieval operation began with the introduction of databanks of chemical, technical, statistical, financial, legal or other company information, where facts and data are recorded in the database and are retrieved directly in response to a user's query. Gradually full text databases came into being where complete texts of documents like directories, encyclopedias, legal cases and correspondences were captured into electronic form, on CD-ROM discs, for example. In such cases, the system is supposed to search the whole text or a particular portion of it in accordance with the given query and should retrieve the particular information sought for.

It, therefore, stands that true text retrieval systems are designed to retrieve information from a database made of any kind of text or data. This capability, in fact, widened the scope of application of text retrieval system. Rowley[11-12] provides a long list of areas where text retrieval software can be applied. In fact, text retrieval packages are useful for any kind of organisation. Major areas are:

Administrative

— Correspondence tracking
— Manual preparation
— Proposals and procedures

Financial

— Credit history
— Capital budget requests
— Business plans

Legal
- Litigation support
- Control analysis
- Brief preparation
- Regulatory findings
- Legislative tracking

Manufacturing
- Project control and planning
- Process description
- Vendor information
- Specifications
- Quality assurance procedures

Marketing
- Competitor analysis
- Customer tracking
- Attitude survey
- Questionnaire analysis
- Product descriptions

Personnel
- Skills inventory
- Resume tracking
- Employee benefit policies
- Self-instruction programs
- Performance reviews

Scientific and engineering
- Technical abstracts
- Journal articles
- Research cross references
- Patent information
- Reaction results

A closer look through the above list would reveal that text retrieval systems are applicable virtually to every area of an organisation, though it includes only a few library/information related activities under the broad heading 'Scientific and Engineering'. One of the most prominent target group of users of text retrieval software is the library and information centres where the normal day-to-day functions relate to bibliographic and information retrieval activities. Therefore, we can supplement the list mentioned above with library and information centres as the most prominent areas of application of text retrieval software. Text retrieval software can be used in libraries for a variety of applications, for example,

— for developing machine-readable and online public access catalogue;
— for developing in-house information retrieval systems;
— for preparation of bibliographies, indexes, printed catalogues, current awareness lists, *etc.*;
— for preparation of biographies, *etc.*;
— for providing various current awareness services, and so on.

The basic nature and objective of a text retrieval system make it different from database management systems (see for detailed discussion Chapter 9). Some of the application areas mentioned above demand database management facilities and it is doubtful whether traditional text retrieval packages are quite efficient in performing those jobs entirely. Nonetheless, keeping our attention towards libraries and information systems, it may be stated that text retrieval systems are quite capable of improving the quality of information service by retrieving the necessary references, and the exact information wherever necessary. Whether text retrieval systems are entirely capable of handling information retrieval and library housekeeping operations as well as the traditional database management or office management requirements in libraries is still a question.

4.8 PROBLEMS ASSOCIATED WITH TEXT RETRIEVAL

Although text retrieval systems have a number of useful features, there are certain issues which need careful consideration while using a text retrieval system. The first step in using a text retrieval system involves defining the database structure. This is one of the most important steps and the future performance of the system depends largely on this. Therefore, while deciding the database structure, the objectives and proposed functions of the retrieval system are to be taken into account.

Once the design aspects have been settled, there come the issues of capturing, verifying, and loading data. Capturing and verifying data are usually application-specific tasks and therefore should depend on the organisation concerned. One important factor is whether the system allows input of standard format data such as MARC records. Some text retrieval systems allow direct loading of standard format data, for example ASSASIN, CAIRS, etc., allow loading of MARC format data, whereas in some cases conversion of data format is necessary before loading the data onto the database, as in the case of CDS/ISIS. Another question relates to capturing of data from a standard word processor which makes the process of data entry much simpler and faster. Some systems allow usage of standard word processor, for example BRS/Search, ideaList, *etc.*, allow to use Multi-Edit for the purpose of data entry.

Updating a database creates problems especially when the number of new or updated records is considerably large. There are different methods for updating a database, *viz.*

— Offline updating;
— Online updating with offline reorganisation;
— Online update file with offline merging; and
— Online updating.

Where currency of data is not a vital issue, the first approach may be taken; this approach will be useful for bibliographic databases. The second approach allows to maintain currency of data, but this occurs at the expense of reduction in retrieval speed. The third approach achieves currency by maintaining two database files, with a corresponding increase in search time. Both these approaches are suitable for applications which need currency of data. The final approach is useful for small database but appears impracticable for large databases. It may be necessary to delete records from a database. This can cause problems because the deleted records may leave gap in the database and it may be difficult to fill in the same with new records.

As the size of the database increases, the efficiency of

the system decreases. For a large text database, the size of the index file(s) will be quite large and it may take long time to locate a given search term. This problem is often tackled by creating several small databases instead of a large one. In a bibliographic database, records can be divided according to date of origin or date of entry into the database. However, in that case, separate search is to be conducted for each database.

It is important to remember that the aim of an information retrieval system is to act as a tool for the user to enable him to carry out his task as easily as possible. The ways in which the user can interact with the system will be just as important as the function that the system provides. There are four main areas where user interface is important, *viz.*,

— Text input;
— Database update;
— Search formulation; and
— Text output.

Text retrieval systems generally lay emphasis on user interfaces which provide better facilities for searching and for producing output. However, facilities should also be available for easy input and editing of records.

4.9 SPECIAL PROBLEMS OF FULL TEXT RETRIEVAL SYSTEMS

The problems mentioned above relate to any text retrieval system. Besides, there are some problems which are specific to full-text retrieval system. Full text retrieval systems are designed to display, as the result of a successful search, the 'facts' directly on the screen from a single source. The major problem of a full text database is that the text should be in ASCII or EBCDIC format which is intelligible to the database handler. Ashford and Willett[13] mention that typical full text systems include transcripts of news items, legal statutes and cases, patents, standards and safety regulations, research programs, product directories, catalogues of engineering components, *etc.*

Acquisition of complete text in the database is often a major problem of full text systems. Keyboarding the whole lengthy text is not only a time-consuming job, but is also quite expensive. An attractive way of entering full texts may be to use the method of Optical Character Recognition (OCR). However, this requires the original text in quite clean and standard fonts. Ashford and Willett[13] estimate that a clean input in a standard font delivers 100 million characters or more of converted text per year, allowing for checking and therefore on a large job this is quite economic in comparison to manual keyboarding of text.

Another problem of full text systems arises from the time and resources taken up in updating following additions of new materials. Need for updating is not quite unexpected given the large size of the text data and the auxiliary files, but it does make frequent amendments quite costly in terms of computer resources.[13]

While discussing the major difficulties associated with text retrieval systems, Basch[14] mentions that a full text database may be a garden of earthly delights, but it is often abundant in snakes. The major problems associated with text retrieval systems are mentioned below.

— Different database designers or online services often handle the same publication differently which may confuse the user community. Again, some services include selected part of the texts for economic use of disk space, but this may hamper user's interest.

— Searching a full text database, especially creation of an accurate search prescription is often a difficult task. It is often difficult to get a balance between recall and precision which depends on usage of correct number of terms and proper combination of them (especially when Boolean operators are used).

— Users often find it difficult to cope with the different ways of formulating search prescriptions and conducting actual searches prescribed by different text retrieval packages. For this, users often have to spend quite a long time in getting used to search a particular database, and experience of using one system may not do well in other. Although, some systems offer online help and tutorial facilities, these are not quite suitable for novice and occasional users.

— In some text retrieval packages the full entry of the hit records are displayed and user often finds it difficult to conclude whether the hit document is useful or not. No doubt, the retrieval system will often retrieve some irrelevant items and the matter will become worse when the user has to spend a large amount of time to judge the relevance. One solution might be to highlight the sought term in the hit record preceded and followed by some other words or terms through which the user can understand the context.

— One major difficulty that arises in text retrieval system relates to the need for typing at the time of searching. The more a user has to type, the more likely he is to produce typos (typographic errors). The same may have occurred at the database creation stage. Quality control should be retrospective as well as current, with imperfect records corrected when the database is updated.

— Quite often an online search vendor provides access to more than one text/IR databases and offers user defined global searching in one form or other. Such a global searching may not always yield satisfactory result due to difference in search strategy of the concerned systems, or due to improperly planned searching by the user.

— Where global searching tries to encompass a number of sources in a single search, source searching simply cares about finding a full text publication online regardless of the system or database on which it is carried.[14] A given publication, *e.g., Financial Times* of London, may be available in more than one online system and may differ in terms of coverage, format, *etc.* It is often difficult for a user to know about the format of the text that a given system handles and to choose one that will suit a particular need. To make a right choice, the user may need to go through the detailed documentation of the systems available to him.

4.10 RECENT IMPROVEMENTS IN THE TEXT RETRIEVAL ENVIRONMENT

There have been many improvements in text retrieval systems since their origin. Some changes relate to database management facilities and provisions for integration with standard database management packages. These issues will be taken up in Chapters 8 and 9 in detail. However, one major change has taken place due to the introduction of CD-ROM. Text retrieval packages can now operate on text databases available on CD-ROM.

Another major improvement has taken place in regard to interfaces with other packages. These interfaces have improved facilities of text retrieval systems by performing the tasks of word processing, statistical and graphical operations with the help of other software package attached through interfaces. Some systems do have an automatic interface, but sometimes interface needs to be created. For example, with INFO-TEXT a tailored interface to library housekeeping systems can be achieved by simple programming.[1]

A great deal of interest in the text retrieval, particularly in full text retrieval market, is placed on retrieval aids. Significant research efforts are made to develop these aids. They are quite sophisticated, and can be categorised into three broad classes,[3] *viz.*

— automatic content analysis and indexing;
— alternate word generation; and
  relevant document evaluation.

Automatic indexing is an attempt to process a document when it is entered into a database and to assign index terms to it so as to facilitate efficient retrieval. Much research efforts were spent during seventies and eighties, in particular for automatic generation of index terms and phrases, and automatic classification of documents based on document clusters, *etc.* These studies were based on statistical analysis of document words and not on the sentences or larger constructs. However, researches are attempting to apply automatic natural language processing techniques for analysing document texts syntactically and semantically (often using pragmatic knowledge also) in order to arrive at an unambiguous representation of the contents of the documents. Discussion on such studies are available widely in literature (see for example, Chowdhury[15-17]).

The most recent and significant research in text retrieval, particularly in the full text retrieval environment, have resulted the developments of knowledge-based systems. These systems aim at automatic analysis of the contents of texts through knowledge-based approaches. Some knowledge-based systems, designed so far, fulfil the dreams of information professionals in the sense that users can get answers to queries presented in a natural language form from a full text database. Chapter 11 of this book is devoted to a discussion on such systems.

REFERENCES

1. J. Rowley, What is Text Retrieval and Why is it Important? In: I. Rowlands, ed. Text Retrieval: an Introduction. London, Taylor Graham, 1987, pp. 1-13.
2. F.N. Tetsky, *Information Retrieval Systems for the Future*, London, The British Library, 1984.
3. M.A. McDonald, Textual Information Management Systems (TIMS): powerful full-text retrieval. In: Proc. of the Ninth National Online Meeting, New York, May 10-12, 1988. pp. 239-245.
4. W. Saffady, *Text Storage and Retrieval Systems: A Technology Survey and Product Directory*, London, Meckler, 1989.
5. M.E. Williams, The State of Databases Today, In: K.Y. Marcaccio, ed., Computer-readable databases: a Directory and Data Sourcebook. Detroit, Michigan, Gale Research Inc., 1989, vii-xiv.
6. H. Dyer and A. Gunson, *A Directory of Library and Information Retrieval Software for Microcomputers*, Ed. 4, Aldershot, Gower, 1990.
7. R. Kimberley, ed., *Text Retrieval: a Directory of Software*, Ed. 3, Aldershot, Gower, 1990.
8. M. Bain, R. Bland, L. Bernard, J. Duke, C. Edwards, D. Lindsay, N. Rossiter and Peter Willett, *Full Text Retrieval Systems: a review and evaluation*, London, Taylor Graham, 1989.

9. N. Firth, *Introduction,* In: I. Rowlands, ed. Text Retrieval: an Introduction. London, Taylor Graham, 1987, pp. iii-iv.
10. A. Ramsden, Why Choose a Text Retrieval Package and What Packages are Available. In: I. Rowlands, ed. Text Retrieval: an Introduction. London, Taylor Graham, 1987, pp. 14-26.
11. J. Rowley, An Overview of the Available Text Retrieval Software, In: R. Kimberley, ed. Text Retrieval in Context: Proceedings of the Institute of Information Scientists Text Retrieval '84 Conference. London, Taylor Graham, 1985, pp. 46-60.
12. J. Rowley, Text Retrieval Software 1985: a Survey of Recent Developments. In: R. Kimberley, ed. Integrating Text With Nontext—a Picture is Worth 1K Words: Proceedings of the Institute of Information Scientists Text Retrieval '85 Conference. London, Taylor Grahm, 1986 pp. 19-35.
13. J. Ashford and P. Willett, *Text Retrieval and Document Databases,* Chichester, Chartwell-Bratt, 1988.
14. R. Basch, The Seven Deadly Sins of Full-text Searching. *Database,* 12(4), 1989, 13-23.
15. G.G. Chowdhury, Natural Language Processing and Information Retrieval. Part I, Basic Issues. *Iaslic Bulletin,* 36(2), 1991, 45-49.
16. G.G. Chowdhury, Natural Language Processing and Information Retrieval. Part II, Major Applications, *Iaslic Bulletin,* 36(2), 1991, 51-59.
17. G.G. Chowdhury, *Information Retrieval Systems,* Calcutta, Iaslic, 1994.

Chapter 5
File Structures for Text Retrieval

5.1 INTRODUCTION

The elementary units of a text retrieval system are the document records. Each document record comprises a number of fields and subfields, each one of which contains a particular unit of information, *viz.*, author's name, publisher's name, title, keyword(s), class number, ISBN, *etc.* The document record may also contain abstract or full text of document. A text retrieval system is designed to provide fast access to the records through any of the sought keys or access points. This means that there should be a mechanism for fast access to the document records.

What should be the basic mechanism for accessing the document records through some key values—by chosen keyword(s), or by author's name, say? To answer this question, we should first understand how are the document records physically stored in the computer. Document records are stored one after another in the computer memory; this is actually the virtual structure of the database file.

Imagine a text database which stores a few, say ten, document records. Now, suppose a user wants to check if there is any document in the database which is written by F.W. Lancaster; another user wants to know if there is any book on telecommunication. How would the user approach? The simplest way would be to open each document record one after another and to check each and every field; if there is a match then retrieve that document. This process continues till all the document records have been checked. This may be a very simple approach, but one can very well imagine that this will be an extremely slow process even for a faster computer when the text database is relatively large and will be an impossible proposition for a database that have some hundred or thousand document records or more.

What is the solution then? How can we retrieve the desired document records? Let's take a common example. What do we do when we want to locate a particular term or phrase, say the word 'computer', or the phrase 'information retrieval', in a book? Do we start from the first line in the first page and continue upto the last line in the last page of the book? The emphatic answer is no. Rather we use a simple tool—the back-of-the-book index.

What is a back-of-the-book index? It is a simple alphabetical list of all the potential index terms, drawn from the text of the book, each having a pointer showing the occurrence(s) of the terms. Thus, we look into the index file with the required search term, locate it and then move to the referenced page for actual information. A similar approach is taken in a text retrieval system; an index file is created which contains all the potential index terms arranged alphabetically. This index file is called 'inverted file'. Users looking for a particular information are required to consult the inverted file first which then leads to the main database where the document records are stored.

5.2 INVERTED FILE

In an inverted file system of text retrieval, each database consists of two files. One is the text file which contains what we would expect to find, that is, the document records in their normal form—the form in which they are entered into the database. The other is the inverted file which contains all the index terms, drawn automatically from the document records according to the indexing technique adopted for the purpose. Each index term in the inverted file is associated with a pointer which shows the record number in which the index term occurs.

The indexing technique, i.e., the technique adopted to draw index terms from the records, determines the order in which index terms will appear in the index file. Different techniques may be required for the purpose, for example, the user may want to prepare index entries for

— each and every term occurring in a given field, for example, all the words occurring in the title field; However, there is a risk; some unwanted terms like 'a', 'an', 'and', 'the', *etc.*, occurring in the document titles may also be indexed. To avoid this problem, text retrieval systems usually allow to use stopword file which discards all the unwanted terms from being indexed;

— the whole field as it is, for example, the full title, as they occur in the document records;

— each occurrence of a repeatable field, for example, names of all the authors;

— some selected words or phrases from a field or subfield, for example, some terms and phrases occurring in the title fields; *etc.*

Thus, for each significant index term in the database the inverted file contains an entry along with a 'reference list' which specifies position(s) in the database where that term appears. Therefore, in an inverted file system, the searcher first consults the index file which then refers to the position in the main text database where the desired record appears. Inverted file system is, thus, an example of 'indirect file access'. If the terms are arranged alphabetically in the inverted file, then the file represents an example of 'indirect sequential file organisation.'

Figure 5.1 (a and b) presents a simple example of such an inverted file. Index entries are drawn from all the four sample document records for the author, title, publisher, and keyword fields. Titles have been indexed as it is, while each occurrence of the author and the keyword field in the document records have been indexed.

Figure 5.1 (a and b) shows the essence of an inverted file approach; a user looking for a term 'Expert systems' will retrieve two records, viz., document numbers 3 and 4 from the database, while another user looking for a book written by 'Thrap, A.' will retrieve the book number 2. A complex query with more than one search term combined by Boolean operators with follow the same path. For example, a user with a query 'Expert systems OR File organisation' will retrieve all the four document records, while the other with a query 'Artificial intelligence AND Knowledge-based systems' will retrieve the document record number 3. In the first example, as the search terms are joined by the operator logical 'OR', the system will consult the inverted file for each term and then will merge the document numbers retrieved in each case, while in the second case, because the terms are joined by the logical operator 'AND', the retrieved document numbers for both the terms will be matched to locate the common document numbers, that is, the ones where both the terms are present.

DOCUMENT RECORDS

Document No: 1
Author: Cunninghm, M.
Title: File structure and design
Publisher: Chartwell-Bratt
Year: 1985
Keywords: File structure; File organisation

Document No: 2
Author: Tharp, A.
Title: File organisation and processing
Publisher: John Wiley
Year: 1988
Keywords: File structure; File organisation

Document No: 3
Author: Ford, N.
Title: Expert systems and artificial intelligence
Publisher: Library Association
Year: 1991
Keywords: Expert systems; Artificial intelligence; Knowledge-based systems

Document No.: 4
Author: Charniak, E.; McDermott, D.
Title: Introduction to artificial intelligence
Publisher: Addison-Wesley
Year: 1985
Keywords: Artificial intelligence; Expert systems

Figure 5.1a: Sample Document Records

Index File
Addison-Wesley 4
Artificial intelligence 3, 4
Charniak, E. 4
Chart-Well Bratt 1
Cunningham, M. 1
Expert systems 3, 4
Expert systems and artificial intelligence 3
File organisation 1,2
File organisation and processing 2
File structure 1, 2
File structure and design 1
Ford, N. 3
Introduction to artificial intelligence 4
John Wiley 2
Knowledge-based systems 3
McDermott, D. 4
Tharp, A. 2

Figure 5.1b: Sample Inverted File

5.3 ACCESS TO INVERTED FILES

One important issue for the inverted file system is the size of the index file. If each and every term occurring in the document database is indexed then size of the index file will be too large, equal to that of the main document database. As mentioned earlier, the easiest approach to consult an inverted file is the sequential access method, that is, looking for each index term one after another from the beginning till

— either the sought term is found, or
— key with larger key value is reached, or
— the end of the index file is reached.

However, the time taken for a sequential search depends on two factors, *viz.*

— the key value of the sought key, because the placement of the key will be based on its key value, and
— the length of the index file.

Therefore, a sequential search for a large inverted index

file is a very slow process. In an ordered sequential file, an average n/2 (n denoting the total number of index terms in the file) searches are to be conducted to accomplish a successful or an unsuccessful search. Thus, the number of search probes increases with increase in the value of n. Sequential method of file access is, therefore, not adopted in inverted file-based text retrieval systems. A number of different methods have been developed to reduce the number of search probes, thereby reducing the search time in a text database.

5.3.1 Alphabetic Chain

One way to reduce the number of search probes in an ordered sequential file organisation is to use alphabetic chain.

What is an alphabetic chain? Let's take a simple example. What do we do when we look for a term in a dictionary? Let's suppose that we are looking for the term 'psychology'. Do we start from the beginning of the dictionary? The answer is an emphatic 'no'. Instead, we start from the alphabet 'P', thereby skipping the other alphabets. Within 'P' also we skip some parts dealing with terms beginning with 'pa', 'pb', *etc.*, and start looking for words beginning with 'pr', or 'ps', and then search for the words sequentially. Thus, what mechanism do we follow? We follow some indexes in order to skip some part of the index file so as to reduce the number of words to be searched.

Let's take another example, this time from a library catalogue. What would we do if we had to look for the term 'telecommunication' in a manual library catalogue? We would start our search from the drawer holding cards those start with the alphabet 't'. Then we would follow other tags, if any, to skip some parts of the catalogue file, and selecting the one where we would expect to find the sought term, the range with a tag 'te—tr', say. Thus, there is a mechanism for filing of catalogue cards to facilitate the process of searching. The mechanism is an alphabetic chain which leads us to particular blocks, one after another, till we reach a probable location for the sought term.

In an alphabetic chain, if you are looking for a term beginning with 'A', then you take the first block; if it begins with 'B', then you begin with the second block, and so on. For example, if you are looking for a term 'CAT', you take the third pointer from the first list, and then the first one from the list that is pointed to, and so on. Thus, you would continue down the chain of pointers until the sought term is found or a term is reached whose key value is greater than the term sought in which case the search term does not occur in the index file; in this process you avoid searching a major part of the index file, thereby reducing the search time to a large extent.

One problem with alphabetic chain is that in a subject field many such terms occur whose key values or alphabetic positions are very close to one another, e.g., computation, computations, computational, computer, computers, computerisation, *etc.* It is stated that these terms are in the 'densely populated' area of the alphabet. The trouble is that if most words are in the densely populated area of the alphabet, most of the searches take six or seven probes to locate the sought term.[1-2] The problem could be solved if we had some means to spread over the densely populated parts of the alphabet[1,2,3] so that all the terms could be accessed in more or less the same time.

5.3.2 Binary Search

We have already seen that for a large index file sequential search is quite a time-consuming process. Hence, we would call a search technique better if we could somehow reduce the number of probes required in conducting a search. If we have an ordered file of index terms, we can reduce the number of probes needed to retrieve an index term by applying a binary search technique.

As the term binary suggests the basic mechanism followed is—

> "Automatically divide the search file into two parts at successive level and thereby reduce the number of search probes."

A binary search compares a key of the sought term with the middle record which is identified automatically, then either the sought term is located or half of the file is eliminated for further consideration. The process of elimination is governed by a simple logic—if the sought term is smaller than the middle term then the right half is eliminated and further search is conducted with the left half. Similarly, if the sought term is larger than the middle term, then the first half is discarded and the second half is considered for further search. This process continues till the sought term is found or only one term in the file is left out in which case the search is an unsuccessful one. Figure 5.2 presents the algorithm for the binary search mechanism.

```
Begin
   lower = 1; upper = n;
   while lower <= upper do
            begin
               middle = (upper + lower) div 2;
               if key [sought] = key [middle] then
                     term is found
               else
               if key [sought] > key[middle] then
                     lower : = middle + 1
               else
                     upper : = middle — 1;
            end;
end;
```

Figure 5.2: Binary Search Algorithm

Let's take a simple example to show how the principle of binary search works. Suppose, we have a list of ten keywords as follows:

<u>List of Keywords</u>

communication computation computational computer data dictionary information inforametrics network software

Now, suppose we are looking for the term 'network'. In a simple sequential search we have to make nine search probes to locate the term. Let's see how many probes will be required in a binary search.

Step 1

To begin with, lower is 1 and upper is 10. Hence , the middle is 5 [(1 + 10) div 2 = 5 (fractions are not considered)]. Hence, first we match our search term with that in the fifth position in the list, *i.e.*, 'data'.

communication		dictionary
computation		information
computational	**[data]**	informetrics
computer		network
		software

Our search term, *i.e.*, 'network' has a key value larger than that of the middle term. Hence, we discard the first half and the 'lower' now becomes 6 (see the algorithm: lower: = middle + 1).

Step 2

We, therefore, discard the first half of the file and concentrate on that half having five terms beginning with the term 'dictionary'. The middle term now is the one in position 8 [middle: = (lower, *i.e.*, 6 + upper, *i.e.*, 10) div 2], that is 'informetrics'.

dictionary	**[informetrics]**	network
information		software

Again, the search term has key value larger than that of the middle term and thus left half is discarded and search is conducted on the right side of the file.

Step 3

Lower is now the term in position 9, *i.e.*, 'Network' (Lower = Middle + 1, *i.e.*, 8 + 1 = 9).
The middle term is now 'network' [middle = (lower, *i.e.*, 9 + 10 (upper)) div 2 = 9].

[network]	software

Here, we note that the search term matches with the middle term, and therefore the search ends successfully.

Thus, we have required 3 searches to locate the search

term as compared to 9 searches required in a sequential search. The number of searches to be conducted in a binary search is of the order O ($\log_2$ n), where n denotes the total number of index terms in the file.[1, 4]

3.5.3 Binary Search Tree

One problem with the binary search technique is that at each stage the system has to determine the middle term and then only it can continue to search. This could be avoided if there was a mechanism by which we could organise all the terms in the index file based on their key values in such a way that at each stage only two options would be available and the system could proceed by making only one comparison. Binary search tree is such an organisation where all the key values smaller than that of the current node, are stored in its left tree and the larger ones are in its right tree.

To conduct a search in a binary tree, we start at the root node of the tree (that is the node at the top of the tree) and then we proceed either to the left or to the right subtree depending on the value of the sought key and that of the node. This process continues till we find a match or we reach a leaf node, that is, a node which does not have a branch, in which case we declare it as an unsuccessful search. Figure 5.3 provides a simple example of a binary search tree organisation.

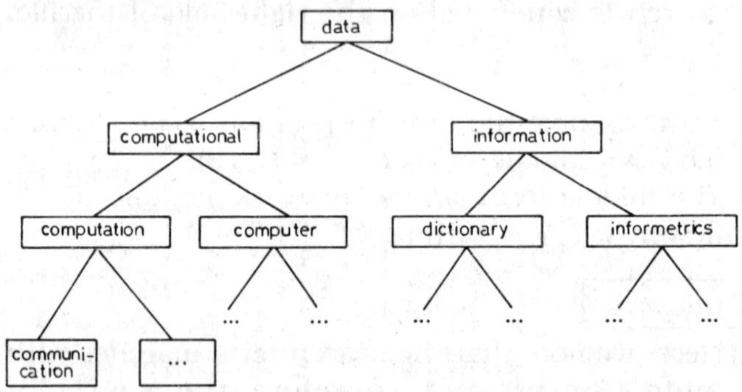

Figure 5.3: Sample Binary Search Tree

It may be noted that the structure of a binary search tree is dependent on the order of insertion of index terms. As the number of terms increases, the depth of the tree increases and, therefore, more number of searches are required to locate a particular term, especially if it happens to occur at the bottom part of the tree. In fact, the maximum number of key comparisons needed to conduct a binary tree search is equal to the longest path from the root to a leaf of the tree.

Insertion of a new term other than in a leaf node (that is a blank space suitable for an inserton) and deletion of a term from the tree sometimes requires a major reshuffle of the tree. In fact, node deletion in a binary tree is more complicated than node searching or node addition because the proper tree structure must be preserved when a node is deleted.

5.3.4 Balanced Tree (B-tree)

A B-tree or a balanced tree, in contrast with a binary tree, is a multiway search tree. As we have already seen in Section 5.3.3, a binary tree has a branching factor of two. A balanced tree does not have a theoretical limit to branching factors. A binary tree grows downwards as new terms are added, whereas a B-tree grows upwards with increase in size.

The structure of a B-tree organisation looks like a multi-branched tree; at each branch point there is a list of index terms, each one with an accompanying pointer. Thus, with this organisation, you find the word which occurs soonest after the one you are searching for in the alphabet. You then follow the corresponding pointer which leads to the next block down in the tree, and there again a pointer is met. Thus, after a few moves you reach the bottom (leaf) node where you find the reference list for the sought term; if the sought term is not found there then it does not occur in the index file and therefore it leads to an unsuccessful search. Figure 5.4 provides a simple illustration of a B-tree.

The composition of a B-tree node is similar to a bucket or a block in that it also contains multiple entries. The number of records that may be stored depends on its capacity order which is specified in the formal definition of the B-tree. Typically the capacity order of a B-tree is between 50 to 200.[1] Each node contains a key value with two associated pointers. The left pointer points to a key of lower key-value while the right pointer points to a key of higher key-value. Since leaf nodes do not have any offspring, they are associated with Null Pointer(^). A B-tree of capacity order one has nodes with one or two keys and two or three pointers.[1]

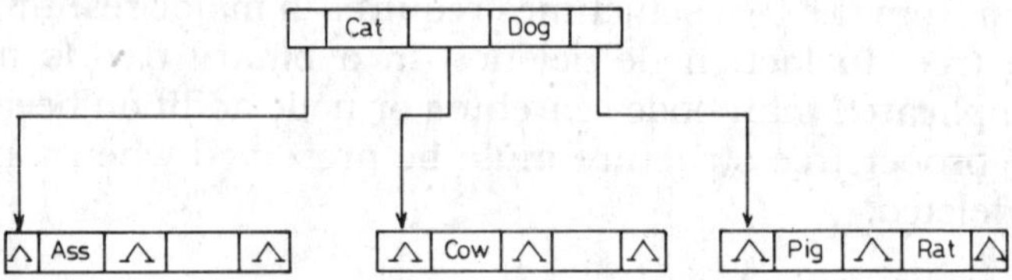

Figure 5.4 B-tree of Order One

Suppose, we want to conduct a search for the index term 'Rat'. We first compare it with the root word, that is 'Cat'. Since the key value of the search term is larger than that of the node, we then compare the search term with the term placed right to it, that is 'Dog'. We do not find a match but we get a pointer to another term with a key value 'Pig'. Upon comparison we find that the search term has a key value which is higher than this term, and thus we move to the right of the term already searched, there we find another term with a key value 'Rat'. Here, we find a match and thus come to the end of a successful search.

Figure 5.5 shows another example of a B-tree where one term has been added to that represented in Figure 5.4. Let us consider how it is inserted. We start with the B-tree shown in Figure 5.4. We want to insert the term with a key value 'Goat'. We follow the same route as we did in conducting a search. We begin with a comparison with the first key in the root, that is 'Cat'. As our term has a larger key value, we move to the right and make a comparison with the key 'Dog'. Here, we find a pointer which leads us to the key 'Pig'. Our term has a lower key value than that met here. Thus, the term 'Goat' maps to the leaf node with 'Pig' and 'Rat'. Because that node is full, we have to split it. The key with the term 'Pig' is elevated to the root level, and one leaf node is split into two nodes. Now since the root node is full (the one with the key values 'Cat' and 'Dog'), there is no room for the elevated record 'Pig.' Thus, that root node is split into two, whereby the key value 'Dog' is elevated to root node having two leaf nodes accommodating two key values—one with 'Cat' being smaller takes the left path, whereas the key with 'Pig' takes the right path. The B-tree formed thus is shown in Figure 5.5.

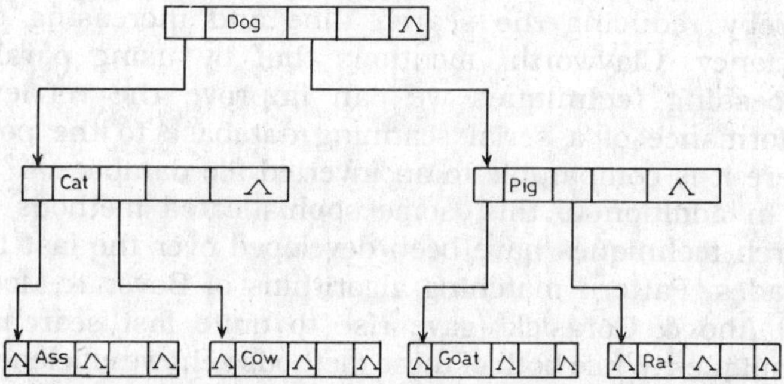

Figure 5.5: B-tree of Order One (after insertion of the key 'Goat')

The advantage of the B-tree mechanism is that the number of file access needed to reach a reference list is the number of levels in the tree. Because the blocks are always split rather than having new branches added at the bottom of the tree, new levels are not created until it is absolutely necessary. This actually helps reduce the average retrieval time.

5.4 ALTERNATIVE TEXT RETRIEVAL STRUCTURES

The easiest way to search a term in a text database might be to compare the given term with each and every term in the text file taking one at a time; but this is practically impossible. The inverted file system has been designed for this purpose. With the alphabetic chain or tree searching technique access to the inverted file may be easier and less time-consuming but these methods have other problems. Major problems arise when the database needs updating. A number of changes need to be made in the file access methods whenever any new term needs to be incorporated into or deleted from the alphabetic chain or the tree. In case of simple serial scanning, this problem would not appear because any new term could be appended with the existing ones without hampering the existing structure. However, time required for serial scan still remains.

Introduction of parallel processing system has brought much hope in text retrieval world. Scanning of large text files can now be performed with parallel processors and thereby reducing the search time and increasing the efficiency. Clayworth[2] mentions that by using parallel processing techniques we can improve the retrieval performance of a serial scanning database to the point where it is comparable to an inverted file database.

In addition to this, some sophisticated methods for search techniques have been developed over the last two decades. Pattern matching algorithms of Boyer & Moore and Aho & Corasick[5] gave rise to quite fast searching techniques. While both of these methods achieve efficiencies in operation by reducing the number of characters in each document which need to be matched against the query patterns, another approach called the text signature approach to serial text scanning tries to eliminate some of the documents in toto from the pattern matching search.[1, 4, 7, 8]

5.4.1 Text Signature

A record signature or a text signature is an encoding of the contents of records or lines of text to characterize its essence.[1] A text signature is a function that transforms text words into integers in the range $[0, 2^b - 1]$, where b corresponds to the number of bits of the signature; it is important that the transformation function spreads the signatures uniformly in the given interval.[8] It may be noted that as the number of words in the text is generally much bigger than the number of possible integers that can be generated by the hash function, different words may be transformed to the same signature causing the possibility of false drops. This problem, however, can be controlled by the signature length b.[8]

Text signature method works by dividing the file into blocks, each of which contains no more than some fixed number of words. Associated with each block, in a separate file is a bit pattern which is also of fixed size. In its implementation, text signatures contain bits of information; its length is usually a multiple of the computer word size to allow efficient processing. In adding text signatures to the records of a file, we actually preprocess the data so as to minimise the retrieval time. Thus, when we look for an information, we generally match the bit pattern of the sought term(s) with the text signature (Figure 5.6).

Signatures	Text records
01101010	....
10000101	....
10010101	....
01101010	....
10001110	....
11101110	....
00100011	....
11000110	....
10101001	....
00010011	....

Figure 5.6 Text File with Signature Added

How are the bit patterns formed then? The basic objective is to use a mechanism by which key values can be converted to key addresses so that while searching a given key, a particular location in the computer memory can be accessed to find that key. For every word a hashing algorithm is used to generate a bit pattern in which a certain fixed number of bits are set. Now for each block the pattern of set bits is generated by combining together the bit patterns for the words in that block, using the Boolean OR function.

Suppose, the bit patterns for some index terms have been generated as follows:

Bananas	00100010
Apples	00100100
Nuts	01000100
Sugar	01000010
Ice cream	01000001
Chocolate	10000100
Vanilla	10000010

By superimposing the codes for the terms we can generate text signatures as follows:

Ice cream	01000001
Chocolate	10000100
Chocolate ice cream	11000101
Ice cream	01000001
Vanilla	10000010
Vanilla ice cream	11000011
Apples	00100100
Bananas	00100010
Nuts	01000100
Mixed fruits	01100110

Now , out of these three signatures if we want to know in which 'chocolate' is a component, we have to take the bit pattern of 'chocolate' and compare with the text signatures to check if we have '1's in the same positions in any of the signatures as that of 'chocolate'. 'Chocolate' has '1's in one and sixth positions and thus we would retrieve 'Chocolate ice cream' because it has '1's in one and sixth positions.

What happens when we are looking for 'Nuts'? The code for this term has '1's in the second and the sixth positions. Therefore, for obvious reasons we would retrieve 'Mixed fruits', because its signature has '1's in the second and sixth position. However, at the same time we would also retrieve 'Chocolate ice cream' because its signature also has '1's in the second and sixth positions. Similarly, while looking for the term 'Sugar', we would have a hit (for 'Vanilla ice cream' because it has '1's in the second and the seventh positions), though none of the signatures contain the sought term. These are 'false drops'.

Why do we have false drops? It is because when we condensed the coded information, we lost something; we no longer have the exact information. One way to reduce the number of false drops is to increase the code size from eight to sixteen bits.

Why is the signature matching a very fast process? It is because in signature matching what we basically do is the matching of bits of information. All computers have special built-in mechanisms for processing entire bit strings in a single operation. The compaction factor is also an important issue because by developing text signatures, we reduce the size of text files to a significant extent. Typically a text signature file is about 10% of the size of the actual text file that it represents (compare it with inverted index files which is about the same size of the text file, *i.e.*, 100%), and the probability of false drops in a good text signature method is even less than 1%.[2] Thus, with the help of text signature, the search time can be reduced to 10%, because the time to search a file is proportional to the amount of text it has to read.

REFERENCES

1. Alan Tharp, *File organisation and processing*, New York, John Wiley, 1988.
2. David Clayworth, File structures for text retrieval. In: Peter Gillman, ed. Text retrieval: the state of the art, London, Taylor Graham, 1990, pp. 141-158.
3. Margaret Cunningham, *File structure and design*, Chichester, Chartwell-Bratt, 1985.
4. R.S. Boyer and J.S. Moore, A Fast String Searching Algorithm. *Communications of the ACM*, Vol. 20, 1977, 762-772.
5. A.V. Aho and M.J. Corasick, Efficient String Matching: an aid to Bibliographic Search. *Communications of the ACM*, Vol. 18, 1975, 333-340.

6. R. Sedgewick, *Algorithms*, Ed. 2, Wokingham, Addison-Wesley, 1988.
7. G. Salton, *Automatic Text Processing: the Transformation, Analysis, and Retrieval of Information by Computer*. Reading, MA, Addison-Wesley, 1989.
8. J. Ashford and P. Willett, *Text Retrieval and Document Databases*, Chichester, Chartwell-Bratt, 1988.
9. D.E. Knuth. *The Art of Computer Programming. Vol. 3, Sorting and Searching*. Reading, MA, Addison-Wesley., 1973.

Chapter 6
Choosing a Text Retrieval Software

6.1 INTRODUCTION

Text retrieval systems began to appear from early seventies. Since then a number of software packages for text retrieval appeared in the market. However, while most of the systems have been designed with universal applicability, some have come up keeping a particular domain in mind. Having all these text retrieval software packages all around, it is difficult to pick up the right software. This chapter addresses the basic issues to be considered while choosing an appropriate text retrieval software.

6.2 BASIC REQUIREMENTS

A pre-requisite to choosing a text retrieval software is the understanding of the actual requirements of the organisation. This section points out some of the most common issues which should be settled before going to choose a particular software. All these issues relate to the specific requirements of the organisation where the text retrieval software will be installed.

6.2.1 Functionality

Functionality is a very important question in regard to the choice of a software.[1] Noerr[2] mentions that all of the following tasks are regarded as text retrieval operations but they are in essence different in terms of functionality:

— generation of a mailing list;

— conducting different kinds of searches;

— information manager to handle notes, articles; *etc.*

The second question relating to functionality is the nature of data to be handled. It is to be decided what kind of data is to be handled by the proposed system, *viz.*, unstructured documents, structured records, only text or text with graphics, and so on. The nature of data is one of the most important determinant factors. This is again related to the nature and format of the output wanted.

The third issue relates to the kind of searches to be conducted. The basic questions to be considered include

— what are the fields to be searched,
— what types of searches are to be performed,
— whether search refinement would be necessary,
— whether search is to be restricted within one or more fields,
— whether free-text search will be permissible, and so on.

Other important factors include the nature and format of the output to be produced. The following questions are involved here:

— whether the search output is to be a ranked list,
— whether frequency of occurrence of the search terms would be necessary,
— whether percentage of search results is to be displayed, and moreover
— whether the output is to be produced in a user defined format.

All these questions relate to the functionality of the system and are to be answered beforehand.

6.2.2 Performance

Having considered the nature of work that the software is supposed to perform, it is desirable to determine how efficiently it should do it. This aspect is related to the software speed. There is another important factor for a text retrieval software—the 'response time', which is the time from a user's typing of a query to the time when the system provides a response, even unsatisfactory. Some systems display the result of progress since a query is presented while some systems simply go on processing and response is not provided until the search is finished. Such systems often baffle the user especially when the user has to sit at the terminal for a considerably long time. Similar is the case for displaying results. Some systems provide options to the user to go either for brief output or the whole of the retrieved document. The latter one takes quite a long time, especially when the documents are quite long and the number of retrieved output is large. In most cases a brief output serves the user's purpose and, therefore, he does not want to waste a long time by going through the whole document that has been retrieved. Again, it is to be determined how easily a search can be conducted, which raises issues like whether it is a menu-based or command-driven system; whether WIMP (Windows, Icons, Mouse & Pulldown Menus) can be used, and so on.

6.2.3 Size

The nature of works expected from a software determines its complexity as well as size. Normally, systems with sophisticated interfaces tend to take more disk space. Again, size of the database is an important factor. Text databases do not only take large disk space but they also cause large overhead for index and other auxiliary files. Size of the database to be handled, its future growth, and nature of the organisation's changing demands are the important factors to be considered.

6.2.4 Users

Finally, nature and number of users are the factors to be considered before choosing a software. Issues like whether the system will be a single-user system or a multi-user one are to be considered first. Other issues may include questions like how does the software react when more users are added to the system; firstly, does the system permit it? Similarly, it is important to know whether data entering or database creation and searching can be performed parallely.

6.3 CRITERIA FOR EVALUATION OF TEXT RETRIEVAL SOFTWARE

The correct selection of text retrieval software is not trivial. Ascertaining the needs of the organisation is, of course, a pre-requisite and it sets the basic background. However, there are many issues which need to be taken into consideration. There are numerous published literary sources describing the criteria for evaluation of text retrieval packages.[2-11] Following are some important factors which are to be considered at the time of choosing a text retrieval software.

6.3.1 Size and Number of Files

The size of the proposed database will influence the choice of both hardware and software. With the increasing speed and power of micros, microcomputer software is becoming more cost-effective and competitive. However, single-user microcomputer systems often restrict the database size and access; a multi-user approach is needed. A solution is to have a Local Area Network (LAN), but in that case it needs to be ascertained whether the software can be installed on the network or not.

6.3.2 Cross-file Searching

Cross-file searching is often necessary in a text retrieval environment. For bibliographic retrieval purposes this may be required for providing Current Awareness Service (CAS), Selective Dissemination of Information (SDI), *etc.*, where more than one file are to be looked at simultaneously. Similarly, database management operations in libraries will call for cross-file searching.

6.3.3 Menu-driven *Vs.* Command-driven

Some text retrieval packages are menu-driven while some are command-driven. Menu-driven systems are especially suitable for novice users. In a command-driven system, the user has to learn all the necessary command or has to look for 'help' every time. However, performance speed is higher in command-driven systems.

6.3.4 Online Help

An important feature to consider, keeping the users in view, is the availability of 'help' information on the screen. Such help should be available to the users from any point of the software. Some packages also provide online tutorial facilities which help to learn the system quickly.

6.3.5 Complex Search Facilities

Text retrieval systems are characterised by a wide variety of search facilities. Following search facilities should usually be offered by text retrieval packages.

1. Logical and relational expressions
   a. Boolean operators: AND, OR, NOT
   b. Relational operators: limit (=), less than (<), greater than (>), and a combination of these
2. Search controlled vocabulary terms
   a. Enter terms directly
   b. Browse through dictionary file and/or online thesaurus
3. Field defined searching, *e.g.*, title, author, journal, address, abstract, etc., in single field and/or multiple fields
4. Truncation and wild card characters: right, left, variable characters (*e.g.*, *, ?), drop final(s)
5. Proximity searching: terms next to each other, terms within the same sentence, terms within the same paragraph, and terms with the same record.

What is really needed in a text retrieval environment is complex search facilities. This is possible by nested boolean logic where search expressions formed by combination of boolean operators are enclosed in brackets and combined with other bracketed terms, *e.g.*, (library OR documentation) AND (computer OR automation).

6.3.6 Thesaurus Facilities

Provision of a thesaurus enables user to extend or refine a given search to obtain better results. Although, a thesaurus or authority file on a large number of subjects often becomes quite large and thus causes a large overhead, user often benefit from thesaurus facilities.

6.3.7 Search on Range, Date and Class Number

In a library environment, search on a range of date and class number is quite often required. Limiting searches by date and sorting chronologically or numerically can be a very important feature in some applications. Some packages also offer facilities for simple calculations based on numeric values.

6.3.8 Current Awareness Service

Automatic current awareness service is an important requirement in a library environment. Many packages now-a-days allow users to store search strategies, for current awareness purposes, which can be modified as needs change.

6.3.9 Flexible Output

Search results can be printed in any text retrieval software, but what is required is to produce the output in a suitable format. Some text retrieval packages enable users to define the format for printing. Users can also specify the fields to be printed, their order, page set up, headings, and particular print set up like bold, underlined, *etc.*

6.3.10 Import/Export Facilities

Often the search results need to be stored in a separate file for future reference. In a text retrieval environment, user may want to create the database in a separate file and then to load it to the main database. This is a common practice in the working environment of a library. So, in the first case what is required is the ability to export a file while in the second case it is to import a file. These facilities are thus commonly addressed as Import/Export facilities.

6.3.11 Separate Optical Storage Device

As a measure to release the load of hard disk with the text database, some text retrieval packages offer facilities where data can be read from a separate storage device, like CD-ROM or WORM (Write Once Read Many Times) drive. However, one disadvantage here is that response times on optical disc are slow, and therefore, the resulting performance of the text retrieval system will be low.

6.3.12 Index Overheads

All text retrieval systems based on inverted files require large disk storage overheads for the inverted index file, sometimes 2 or 3 fold, depending on exhaustiveness of the indexing strategy. If a microcomputer with limited storage is to be used, then systems which can compress the index files may have to be considered.

6.3.13 Security

Data security is an important issue in almost all organisations. Hence, while choosing a text retrieval system attention should be paid to this, and a system which provides adequate data security should be preferred.

6.3.14 Software Support

Necessary support from the software manufacturer and/or supplier is an important issue and this is to be considered with due importance. Often software manufacturers bring out different versions with some improvements or with corrections of earlier mistakes/bugs. Whether new versions will be available, and if so at what cost, needs to be known, because for an operational system software maintenance and updating is a major problem. At the same time training facility is needed to support the customer. In fact, there are a number of issues related to the reputation of the vendor and software support available from them. Following are the major considerations:

- Experience in marketing to libraries;
- Business and support record which involve questions like
  a. How long in business, how financially sound, and how many installations?
  b. What is the level of product support?
  c. Whether reference sites are available for discussion and visit, *etc.*
- Provisions for on-site assistance;
- Provisions for frequent and substantial product updates;
- Provisions for customer training;
- Provisions for telephone assistance;
- Sponsorship for a user group or newsletter;
- Willingness to participate in on-site demos, etc.

6.3.15 Multi-lingual Versions

Few text retrieval packages have multi-lingual facilities. For example, three dialogue languages, *viz.*, English, French, and Spanish, available in CDS/ISIS.

6.4 QUESTIONS TO BE ASKED

Nieuwenhuysen[12] identifies seven major sets of criteria to evaluate and select software for online text information storage and retrieval, *viz.*

1. Input of Information;
2. Indexing;
3. Interactive information retrieval;
4. Output facilities;
5. SDI/CAS;
6. Cheaper, limited versions, if any; and
7. Integration with other packages.

A number of considerations are involved with each of the above seven categories. Following are the major questions (covering all the seven categories) which could be asked while choosing a text retrieval software:

1. Is it possible to input data through the keyboard?
2. Does the program offer a module for word processing?
3. Does the program allow batch input of files from diskette, magnetic tape, *etc.* ?
4. To what extent can the user define the structure of the database?
5. Can the user link various records in a database?
6. Can the stored information be structured into fields and subfields?
7. Does the program accept repeatable fields or multiple field values?
8. Can the user provide default value for a given field?
9. Can the program automatically control the content of input for specific fields by checking a related file pattern?
10. Does the program offer a thesaurus module which allows the user to store relations among terms used in a database?
11. Are pre-defined existing database structures available

with specific field types, from which user can choose one?

12. What are the limitations concerning input and database structure (like, characters per field, fields per record, characters per record, files per database, number of databases, *etc.*)?
13. Can the user change the content of existing records?
14. Can the user delete existing records?
15. Can the user add new fields into the record structure?
16. Can the user delete fields from the record structure?
17. Can the user change the name or attribute of fields?
18. Can the user change the length of fields?
19. What is the minimum number of:
    a. characters of a term, which are taken up in the index?
    b. terms in a field, which are taken up in the index?
    c. terms in a record, which are taken up in the index?
    d. indexes per database?
20. Can the user use a list of stop words?
21. Can the user use hyphenated words?
22. Does the system allow 'dynamic updating' (input words are immediately indexed) or 'batch updating' (user has to run an indexing program to index the input terms)?
23. How much disk space do the indexes take?
24. How long does it take to create or update index?
25. Can the user choose terms which will be indexed?
26. Are semantic methods available in the program to yield better retrieval by automatically picking up semantically related terms?
27. To what extent can an index be changed or reorganised?
28. Can a list of index terms be displayed on the screen?
29. Does the system allow 'Boolean searching' ('AND', 'OR', 'NOT')?
30. Does the system allow 'proximity searching' (two adjacent terms, two terms with one or more intermediate terms, two terms in a given field or paragraph)?
31. Can parenthesis be used in combination of search

terms to indicate the order?

32. Can wild card be used for indicating truncation at the end of search term?
33. Can a search term be truncated at the beginning?
34. Is embedded truncation (truncation in the middle of a search term) available?
35. Is it possible to use more than one truncation simultaneously?
36. Can the searching be limited to specified field(s)?
37. Can the user search for terms which are not included in the index (free-text searching)?
38. Can the user conduct a phonetic search (when the user is not quite sure about the spelling, for example, in case of names of persons)?
39. Can the user assign weights to search terms?
40. Does the program make distinction between lowercase and uppercase letters in the search terms?
41. Can the user go on with a search on the basis of previous search results?
42. Does the system show the number of times a given search term occurs in a given retrieved record?
43. Does the system show any sort of statistics regarding the occurrence of search terms, retrieved records, *etc.*?
44. Does the system show search history (*i.e.*, search queries produced at different steps)?
45. Can the queries/search strategies be saved?
46. Can the user define how the records should be sorted in the output?
47. What is the maximum number of sort levels?
48. Can the user use additional word(s) to make the output more intelligible?
49. Can the system highlight the search term(s) in the retrieved record(s)?
50. Can the retrieved records be edited?
51. Can the output of a record be cut off automatically if the size of the complete record exceeds a certain threshold?
52. Can the user define the order in which fields should be placed in the records in the output?

53. Can the user produce desired layout for the output?
54. Can the output be saved?
55. Can the software be used to provide SDI/CAS?
56. Can the user conduct mathematical and/or statistical operations with the values of one or more fields across a set of records?
57. Can the user print a certain number of the retrieved records?
58. Can the user use any password?
59. Can the user put any restrictions towards editing/altering records?
60. Can multiple copies of the software be used at the same price?
61. Can the user get multiple copies of manual/documentation?
62. Can the package be integrated with other software packages?
63. Can the system import data from other packages?
64. Can the user write programs for performing additional operations with the software?
65. Can the software be used in more than one language?
66. Can the user produce keyboard macros?
67. Can the user alter the menu(s) provided with the package?
68. Can the user get online (context-sensitive, if possible) help?
69. Does the software provide online tutorial facility?
70. What are the minimum hardware and memory requirements?
71. In case of a micro-version, is it a stand-alone version or can be run on a local area network?
72. What is the price of the package and is it worth that cost (to be determined by the checkpoints mentioned above and on the basis of market report/review)?

6.5 SUMMARY

This chapter provides ample guidelines for choosing a text retrieval software. The basic requirements are more or less same in all kinds of libraries and an understanding of the basic requirements leads to identification of the specific requirements or the functions that the proposed text retrieval system is supposed to perform. A number of points have been mentioned to provide aid in choosing the right software. It may be noted that a given software may not possess all the ideal qualities. What librarians have to do is to assess the merits and demerits of available software on the basis of the guidelines and checklist provided in this Chapter in order to arrive at a comparative figure and to set themselves in a better position for deciding which one is to select.

REFERENCES

1. D. Bawden, Software for Information Management, In: Perspectives in Information Management 1, ed. by C. Oppenheim, London, Butterworths, 1989, pp. 25-62.
2. P. Noerr, Software: What is Needed?. In: Text Retrieval: the State of the Art, ed. by P. Gillman, London, Taylor Graham, 1990, pp. 31-36.
3. R. Kimberley, ed., *Text Retrieval: a Director of Software*, Ed. 3, Aldershot, Gower, 1990.
4. A. Ramsden. Why Choose a Text Retrieval Package and What Packages are Available? In: Text Retrieval: an Introduction, ed. by I. Rowlands, London, Taylor Graham, 1987, pp. 14-26.
5. L. Schultz, Computerized Literature Files, *Medical Electronics*, Sept. 1983, 72-78.
6. M. Rowbottom, First Steps in Choosing Information Retrieval Packages, *Library Micromation News*, Vol. 4, 1984, 13-16.
7. P. Leggate and H. Dyer, The Microcomputer in the Library. III. Information Retrieval from External and Internal Databases, *The Electronic Library*, Vol. 4, No. 1, 1986, 38-49.
8. R. Pollard, Microcomputer Database Management Systems for Bibliographic Data, *The Electronic Library*, Vol. 4, No. 4, 1986, 230-240.
9. D.A. Kemp, *Computer-based Knowledge Retrieval*, London, Aslib, 1988.
10. H. Dyer and A. Gunson, eds., *A Directory of Library and Information Retrieval Software for Microcomputers*, Ed. 4, Aldershot, Gower, 1990.
11. J.H. Ashford, Storage and Retrieval of Bibliographic Records: a Comparison of Database Management System (DBMS)

and Free Text Approaches, *Program*, Vol. 18, No. 1, 1984, 16-45.

12. P. Nieuwenhuysen, Criteria for the Evaluation of Text Storage and Retrieval Software, *The Electronic Library*, Vol. 6, No. 3, 1988, 160-166.

Chapter 7
Developing a Text Retrieval System

7.1 INTRODUCTION

We have already noted in Chapter 4 (Section 4.7) of this book that a text retrieval software can be used in a number of different operations. Considering its use in library and information related activities, we may find that a text retrieval software can be used for

— developing machine-readable catalogue of bibliographic materials;
— developing online public access catalogue;
— developing information retrieval systems;
— preparation of bibliographies;
— preparation of current awareness lists;
— preparation of accession lists;
— preparation of biographic and factual databases relating to persons, institutions, projects, and so on.

For whatever purpose is the software being used, the databases will have to be designed according to the specific needs of the users. Basic considerations relating to the design and development of a text retrieval system are discussed in this chapter. Tasks involved in various stages of design and development of a text retrieval system are also described; examples have been drawn from two text retrieval software, *viz.*, Micro-CDS/ISIS (or Micro ISIS, as it is sometimes referred to in literature), and ideaList.

It may be noted that this chapter does not intend to act as a manual or workbook for any of the packages, and therefore one may notice that some of the features of the packages have not been described. These packages have been chosen to illustrate the basic process of developing a text retrieval system and making use of the same for general information retrieval purposes.

7.2 BASIC CONSIDERATIONS

In most general terms, to run a text retrieval system we need the following:[1]

1. A software package;
2. A processor to execute the programs;
3. Memory to hold intermediate working;
4. Disk storage to hold the data files;
5. Devices for archiving data files to recover from accidental damage or loss of data;
6. Printer(s) to produce hard-copy for different purposes; and
7. Terminal for data input and for controlling the whole process.

Text retrieval packages vary from single programs like ideaList for a micro to very large multi-program systems like STAIRS which require large computers systems. However, like other application programs, text retrieval programs need a processor to execute, data storage facilities on disk, and output on terminals and printers. The programs are stored in files on disk, the user gives commands to load the text retrieval program, the program is read into the memory and begins to work.

In a single user, single tasking system, the operating system allows only a single stream of operations—one user doing a single application. Multi-user systems allow independent users to access the computer without regard to the operations of other users.

There are a number of factors which are to be considered while going to develop a text retrieval system. Some of these issues are independent of any specific text retrieval software. Once these issues are settled, software-specific issues need to be considered. The first question that should be taken into consideration is the functionality of the proposed system. At this stage, objectives of the proposed system are to be determined. It is important to determine the purpose for which the system is being developed, like

- — as an information retrieval system;
- — as an online public access catalogue;
- — as a system for resource sharing; or
- — for any other specific purpose.

It should also be determined whether it will be a stand-alone system or will be working in a network environment.

Once the designer is certain about the functionality of the system, the next questions that should be answered are

— nature of documents/records to be incorporated into the system;
— maximum number of documents/records to be incorporated into the system; and so on.

These questions are very important because they help the designer choose an appropriate text retrieval software. Software impose a limit on the total number of records which can be created and stored in a particular version. An understanding of the nature of the records also help the designer identify the different fields that are to be created. This has also an impact on the choice of the appropriate software because text retrieval software also impose a limit on the length of individual fields and the total number of fields which can be included in a given database.

Nature and number of users are also important factors to be considered. The performance of the proposed retrieval system can reach a satisfactory level only if the requirements of the users are kept in mind right from the beginning of the design stage. In normal library environment, there are two broad categories of users, *viz.*, the library/information personnel, and the end-users. Library and information personnel often act as intermediaries, but they may also act as end-users—seeking information from the system for their use or for taking a decision. For example, library personnel may assist end-users in locating a given book by searching the online catalogue, or may provide answer to a reference query in which case he acts as an intermediary. On the other hand, the library personnel may consult the online catalogue to ascertain the availability of a book in the library's collection and based on that information he decides whether to place order for the book or not; in this case the library staff acts as an end-user. However, interests of the users should be given due importance at the stage of database design. The structure of a database should be made complex only if user's requirements call for that; the basic guidelines should be the utilitarian principles.

Finally, the designer must pay due attention to the availability of resources which include availability of both the hardware and software as well as necessary manpower. Each text retrieval software prescribes a minimum hardware requirement and before choosing a software one must ascertain the hardware facilities available at his disposal. Similarly, while choosing a software it must be ascertained what kind of training will be required to make optimum use of the software, and in case trained manpower is not available to begin with, what training facilities are available.

7.3 DATABASE DESIGN

Designing the database constitutes the first step of developing a text retrieval system. This step involves a number of important decisions and the performance of the resulting system will depend largely on these decisions. As we have already seen, a text retrieval system may be used for a variety of operations—preparation of library catalogues, bibliographies, current awareness lists, biographical lists, and so on. In each of these cases, the nature of the database and consequently the nature, content, and number of fields will differ.

The first step in database design relates to determination of the different fields and subfields, their nature, content, length, and various other attributes. The designer should also know how the users would approach the database for the purpose of retrieving information, how would they like to see the records displayed or printed, and so on.

Thus, we can enlist the following functions which are to be considered at the stage of database design:

— nature of data;
— nature and number of fields and subfields;
— nature of database indexing;
— format for display and printing of data;
— sorting of data while printing;
— entry/editing of data; *etc.*

Depending on the nature of the data/records to be incorporated into the database, the designer enlists the various fields and subfields. For example, the designer may decide to use the following fields for a simple library catalogue:

Author
Title of book
Publisher's name
Place of publication
Date of publication
Price
Call number
Accession number
Keywords

The designer may wish to bring some items of information under one umbrella, giving a common field name, while keeping each item of information in different subfields. For example, the designer may create a field called 'Imprint' having three subfields, each one for 'Publisher's name', 'Place of publication', and 'Date of publication'.

7.4 DATABASE DEFINITION

In CDS/ISIS, tasks involving the definition of various fields and denoting their attributes, etc., come under the 'Database Definition Services'. There are a number of operations here, the first one is the creation of the 'Field Definition Table' (FDT).

Creation of the FDT includes tasks like

— determination of the proposed fields and subfields;
— providing tag for each field;
— naming each field;
— providing various attributes to each field.

If the proposed system is to be used for resource-sharing or to work in a network environment, a standard for database design and format for display of data must be followed. This means that the use of various fields, their tags, attributes, *etc.*, must be followed uniformly by each library. In order to maintain standards, libraries may follow standard coding practices suggested in the CCF, UNIMARC, *etc.* Sur and Chowdhury[2] discuss the development of a bibliographic database in CDS/ISIS using CCF to ensure standardisation in coding practices. Similar measures have been proposed in the IDIN[3] and MIBIS[4] manuals.

In CDS/ISIS the designer has to choose the option

'D — Database Definition Services'

from the 'Main Menu', which leads to a menu where the designer may wish to design a new database or may prefer to change the definition of an existing database. Figure 7.1 provides the 'Main Menu' and Figure 7.2 provides the 'Database Definition Services' menu in CDS/ISIS.

It may be noted from Figure 7.2 that user has to choose the option

'C—Define a New Database'

in order to design the structure of a new database. At this prompt, the user is asked to provide the name of the proposed database, and then the designer gets a blank table as shown in Figure 7.3.

C — Change data base
L — Change dialogue language
E — ISISENT — Data entry services
S — ISISRET — Information retrieval services
P — ISISPRT — Sorting and printing services
I — ISISINV — Inverted file services
D — ISISDEF — Database definition services
M — ISISXCH — Master file services
U — ISISUTL — System utility services
A — ISISPAS — Advanced programming services
X — Exit (to MSDOS)

Figure 7.1 Main Menu (CDS/ISIS, Version 3.0)

L — Change dialogue language
C — Define a new database
U — Modify database definition
I — Re-initialise data base
R — Unlock data base
X — Exit

Figure. 7.2: Data Base Definition Services Menu (CDS/ISIS, Version 3.0)

Tag	Name	Len	Typ	Rep	Delimiters/Pattern

Figure. 7.3: Blank Screen for FDT

The designer has to fill-in each column in the table for each proposed field. The first column denotes 'Field tag', which should be a unique number; all subsequent operations on the proposed database will be based on these field tags. 'Name' denotes the name of the field, 'Len' denotes the maximum length of the field, 'Typ' denotes the specific type/nature (like numeric, alphabetic, alphanumeric , *etc.*) of the field, 'Rep' denotes whether the given field will be repeatable or not, 'Delimiters' denote the subfield delimiters which separate one subfield from another, and 'Pattern' denotes the specific pattern, if any, in which the designer wants to enter data in a given field, for example, the designer may want to specify a format 99-AAA-9999 for entering date in the format '20-NOV-1993'. Figure 7.4 represents a sample FDT for a simple library catalogue database.

Tag	Name	Len	Typ	Rep	Delimiters/Pattern
100	Author	200	X	R	
200	Title	300	X		
300	Imprint	100	X		abc
400	Collation	50	X		
500	Series	200	X		abc
600	ISBN	15	X		
700	Acc. No.	6	N		
800	Keywords	200	X		

Figure 7.4: Sample FDT for a Library Catalogue Database

Thus, through the FDT the designer denotes what should be the contents of different fields and subfields, what should be the nature and attribute of each field, and so on. It may be noted that the details that one has to provide relating to each field at this stage depend on the requirements prescribed by each text retrieval software. The steps shown here are according to the requirements of CDS/ISIS, and they may for obvious reasons vary in other software.

Let us now see how the structure of a database is designed in ideaList. In ideaList record formats are controlled by a small text file called IDEALIST.DEF. A record format in ideaList has a name and a list of field names, types and attributes. IdeaList comes with seven pre-defined record formats, *viz.*

— article,
— book,
— chapter,
— MEDLINE,
— address,
— dictionary, and
— default format having a single field called text.

Each of these pre-defined record types has certain number of pre-defined fields with some attributes associated with each. For example, the pre-defined record type 'article' contains eight fields, *viz.*

— Author,
— Address,
— Title,
— Date,
— Journal,
— Volume,
— Page, and
— Abstract.

ideaList has six field types, *viz.*

— concatenated: for text; line breaks and white spaces will be ignored during printing or exporting;
— free: for text; line breaks and white spaces are preserved during printing or exporting (the default type);
— name: for surnames and initials;
— number: for numbers;
— date: for dates (European, American, or Japanese formats);
— time: for times.

Each field may have one of the following five attributes:

— indexed: field contents will be indexed (default);
— unindexed: field contents will not be indexed;
— mandatory: field must be filled-in;
— picture: format can be specified for field contents;
— overview: default field for search overview feature.

However, one can modify ideaList's record definitions by adding and/or deleting fields or by changing field types and attributes. One can also create one's own formats with any number of fields in any order.

7.5 DATABASE INDEXING

It may be noted that the field attributes in ideaList allow one to tell the system whether a field will be indexed or not. This can also be done in CDS/ISIS, but in a different step. This is an important step in any text retrieval system because this will generate the index file on which searches can be performed. Both CDS/ISIS and ideaList, like other text retrieval systems, create an inverted index file. In ideaList the advantage is that as you enter or edit records, ideaList creates/updates the index file automatically. However, this is not the case with CDS/ISIS. Once new records are created or existing records are edited in CDS/ISIS, one has to create/update the index file by choosing the option

'I—Inverted File Services'

from the main menu and then choosing the appropriate option(s) from the 'Inverted File Services' menu. However, if this is not done, the user is prompted with a message saying that the record has been changed but the inverted file has not been updated, and the user is asked whether he wants to update it or not. If the user responds positively at this prompt, the inverted file is updated automatically.

Now let us see the steps that one has to follow for the purpose of generation of index files in CDS/ISIS. Index file is generated or updated from within the 'Inverted File Services' menu. However, inverted files are generated with the criteria set in the 'Field Select Table' (FST). In the 'Database Definition Services' menu in CDS/ISIS (see Figure 7.5) there is an option

A — Update Field Definition Table
B — Create/Update Worksheet
C — Copy Worksheet Description
D — Delete Worksheet Description
E — Create/Update FST
F — Copy Field Select Table
G — Delete Field Select Table
H — Create/Update Display Format
I — Copy Display Format
J — Delete Display Format
K — List Database Parameter Files
X — Exit

Figure 7.5: Database Definition Services Menu (CDS/ISIS, Version 3.0)

'E — Create/Update FST'

through which the designer can fix the criteria for indexing the database. Initially the designer gets a blank form as shown in Figure 7.6, where 'ID' denotes the identifier, 'IT' denotes the indexing technique, and 'Data extraction format' denotes format in which data will be extracted automatically from the database records for the purpose of indexing.

ID	IT	Data extraction format

Figure 7.6: Blank Table for the FST

In version 2.3 of CDS/ISIS there are five indexing techniques and the user can choose any one for a given field/subfield:

0 — Index entry will be generated for the whole field.
1 — Index entry will be generated for each subfield.
2 — Index entry will be generated for each term(s) enclosed in angular brackets (<......>).
3 — Index entry will be generated for each term(s) enclosed in slashes (/......../).
4 — Index entry will be generated for each individual term in the field/subfield.

In version 3.0 of CDS/ISIS one can use 4 more indexing techniques which allow to specify a prefix for search terms extracted with indexing techniques '1', '2', '3', and '4'; these are numbered '5', '6', '7', and '8', respectively. For example,

1 8 '\TI = \', v24

will index each term of field 24 and prefix each term with TI =.

The data extraction format in CDS/ISIS tells the system how data is to be extracted from the records for the purpose of indexing. The user may want to index

- each occurrence of a repeatable field, as in the case of authors where the data extraction format will be, say, '1 0 (v100/)' (where 100 denotes the field tag for the author field);
- each word of the title, where the data extraction format will be, say, '2 4 v200' (where 200 denotes the field tag for the title field); use of a stopword list will discard unwanted words from being indexed;
- subfield 'a' denoting the name of 'publisher' of the 'Imprint' field, where the data extraction format will be, say, '3 1 v 300 ^ a' (where 300 denotes the field tag for the imprint field), and so on.

Figure 7.7 shows the sample FST for a simple book database. It may be noted that in Figure 7.7

- indexing technique '0' has been used for the author field in order to create index under each author's name,
- indexing technique '4' has been used to draw index entry under each word occurring in the title field (CDS/ISIS allows the use of a stop word list in order to drop unwanted terms from being indexed),
- indexing technique '0' has been chosen to create index entry for the publisher name occurring in subfield 'a' in the 'Imprint' field, and
- indexing technique '2' has been used to draw index entry under each term/phrase occurring within angular brackets in the 'Keyword' field.

ID	IT	Data extraction format
100	0	mhl, (v100/)
200	4	v200
300	0	v300^a
600	0	v600
700	0	v700
800	2	v800

Figure 7.7: Sample Field Select Table

Thus, the criteria for generation of the index file is fixed at this stage. However, the actual index file is yet to be generated. Once records are created (see Section 7.8), the index file is to be generated by using the option 'I — Inverted File Services' from the Main Menu as mentioned at the beginning of this section.

7.6 DATA ENTRY FORM/WORKSHEET

Another important decision involved in the database design stage relates to the creation of data entry format or worksheet which is like a blank form which is used for entering data in the database. In CDS/ISIS the designer has to create a data entry worksheet which is used by the data entry operators for entering data into the database. The system also allows creation of more than one worksheet, any one of which may be called at the time of data entry operation. However, some text retrieval software allow to enter data directly without having to create any format or worksheet for the purpose. For example, in ideaList data can be entered by calling the specific record format name, for example, 'book', 'article', *etc.*, whereupon user gets a blank form with different field names given in the left margin; text can be entered in free format by using either TED, a small text editor that comes with ideaList or by using an external editor.

While designing a new database in CDS/ISIS, once the task of creating the FDT is over, the system automatically leads the designer to the step of creating the worksheet. In fact, the designer first gets a blank screen. For each field defined in the FDT, the user has to create a column which will be used for future data entry purposes. For each field the user has to follow a few steps--he has to provide the field tag, field length, beginning and end of the column for data entry for that field (given in terms of line and column numbers), specific nature of the field like bold, normal, blinking, *etc.*, default value, if any. The task of creating the worksheet completes when appropriate measures for all the fields defined in the FDT have been taken. CDS/ISIS also allows the user to make necessary editing in an already existing worksheet by choosing the option 'B-Create/Update Worksheet' from the 'Database Definition Services' Menu, and then typing the name of the worksheet where editing will be done. Figure 7.8 shows a sample data entry worksheet for a simple library catalogue database.

```
Author________________________________________
Title_____________________________ Imprint ____
________________ Collation __________ Series _
___________ ISBN ________ Acc. No. _________
_______________ Keywords_________________
_________________________
```

(Note: The author field is a scrolling field, allowing repeatable occurrences, whcih could not be shown in this figure).

Figure. 7.8: Sample Data Entry Worksheet in CDS/ISIS

7.7 DISPLAY OF RECORDS

The database designer has to consider how user will expect the records to be displayed at the time of browsing the database or at the time of displaying the records retrieved by a given search. In CDS/ISIS the designer has to specify a format for display of records; thus, database records can be displayed in a user defined format. However, this facility is not available in all text retrieval systems and as a result records cannot be displayed in a desired format. For example, in ideaList records are displayed exactly in the same way as they are created. Figure 7.9 provides a simple example.

In CDS/ISIS design of a display format is an important

task and the designer has to use a combination of a series of codes defined for the purpose. Figure 7.10 provides a simple display format and Figure 7.11 provides a sample record displayed according to that format.

Figure 7.10 and 7.11 represent very simple format for display of records. However, the designer may prefer to make the display format somewhat complex to display the records according to a chosen format, AACR2, say. Figure 7.12 shows a little complex display format and Figure 7.13 shows the corresponding display of record.

Author	G.G. Chowdhury
Address	Dept of Information Studies University of Sheffield Sheffield S10 2TN
Title	Natural language processing and information retrieval
	Part I: Basic issues
Date	1991
Journal	IASLIC Bulletin
Volume	36
Page	45-49
Abstract	

Figure 7.9 Sample Display of Data in ideaList

```
"MFN: "mfn(5)/"Author : "v10(8,9)/
"Title: "v20(7,8)/"Imprint : "v30(9,10)/
"Collation : "v40(11,12)/"ISBN :
"v50(6,7)/"ACC. No. : "v60(11,12)
```

(Note: Field tags: 10 = Author; 20 = Title; 30 = Imprint; 40 = Collation; 50 = ISBN; 60 = ACC. NO.)

Figure 7.10: Sample Display Format (1) in CDS/ISIS

MFN : 01020
Author : Tharp, Alan A.
Title : File organisation and processing
Imprint : New York; John Wiley and Sons; 1988
Collation : xvii, 398p.
ISBN : 0-471-61766-0
ACC. No. : 169520

Figure 7.11: Output of Display Format (1) in CDS/ISIS

```
mhl, v100(0,2)/v200 (2,0),“ /
”v100(0,0),/. —| v300^a“: ”, v300^b“,
”,v300^c“. ”/v400 (2,0)|. — (|“
v500^a(0,0), |, | v500^b(0,0), |; |
v500^c(0,0),“)” d500/ “ISBN ”d600,
v600/“ACC No. ”v700 ”.”/##
```

(Note: Field tags : 100 = Author; 200 = Title; 300 = Imprint (subfields a = Place; b = Publisher; C = Date); 400 = Collation; 500 = Series (subfields a = Series name; b = Series no. ; c = Series editor); 600 = ISBN; 700 = Accession number)

Figure 7.12: Display Format (2) in CDS/ISIS

Suad Alagic
Object-oriented database programming /Suad Alagic.—New York: Springer-Verlag, 1989.
xv, 320 p.—(Texts and monographs in computer science series, no. 1; David Gries)
ISBN 0-387-96754-0
ACC No. 170856

Figure 7.13: Sample Output Corresponding to Display Format (2) in CDS/ISIS

The display format shown in Figure 7.12 is relatively complex but it does not accommodate all those rules and commands which would be necessary to display different kinds of documents having various cataloguing problems. In other words, it does not make provisions for appropriate resolution of the various complexities that may occur in day-to-day cataloguing activities in a library. In an environment of automated cataloguing of monographs the system has to take many decisions for proper display of records,

— when main entry will be under author;
— when main entry will be under title;
— when main entry will be under corporate body;
— when main entry will be under uniform title; and so on.

These decisions are necessary because catalogue codes, like AACR2, prescribe specific rules for display of records for each of the circumstances mentioned above and for many other similar situations. The system has to take various measures for proper indentation of data elements, and for proper use of various appropriate punctuation marks. A complex display format and corresponding display of various records according to AACR2 have been provided by Sur and Chowdhury.[2]

7.8 DATA ENTRY, SEARCHING AND PRINTING

The job of database design ends with the tasks mentioned above. The next job is the creation of records. This involves entering data elements in the appropriate columns in the worksheet or format for data entry. This can be done in one of the two ways. Records can be created by keying-in the data elements in each field and subfield in the data entry form/worksheet, or a number of records can be downloaded from other already existing databases. CDS/ISIS comes with a simple editor which is used for online entry/editing of data. This simple editor allows normal keyboard operations along with basic text editing operations like copying, cutting, pasting, *etc.*

ideaList comes with a similar simple editor, called TED, which can be used for entry or editing of data. However, ideaList allows users to specify any other desired editor for this purpose.

In case of downloading of data from some other sources a few other questions are to be considered, the most important ones being the compatibility of the data format, and the interface program which will convert data created in one format to the other. In CDS/ISIS data can be downloaded from other sources through the ISO 2709 format. IdeaList allows downloading of data from the MEDLINE database in a very simple manner.

Once records are created and/or downloaded, and necessary indexes are generated—either automatically as in case of ideaList or in a batch mode as in case of CDS/ ISIS (through the 'Inverted File Services' menu), users can carry out search operations through the appropriate menu provided by the software for the purpose.

The search output can be displayed on the screen or can be stored in a file for future reference or for printing. The search output can be displayed according to the display format designed for the purpose, if any, or in the default display format given in the software.

Text retrieval software allow users to define the specific format in which records can be printed. In CDS/ISIS this can be achieved through the 'Sorting and Printing Services' menu. Here, users are allowed to sort the output in any order; three sort levels are available, for example,

level 1 : records are first sorted according to author;
level 2 : more than one title by a given author are sorted by title; and
level 3 : more than one of the same title by the same author are sorted by date of publication.

Users will have to fill-in the specific columns in the print and/or sort worksheet for the purpose. The format prepared for display of records on the screen can be accepted as the print format, or a specific format may be designed using the same conventions used for preparing the display format.

In ideaList there is no specific menu option for printing records. Printing in ideaList is a kind of exporting, but done to the printer instead of to a file. Exporting, either to a printer or to a file, is controlled by export format files which specify

— the record types to format;
— the fields that are to be included;
— the order in which the fields will appear;
— the punctuations to be used in between different data elements; and
— text words that are to be used in and around the fields.

Export files in ideaList are picture representations of what one wants the output to look like. For example, the output file:

paper
Author. Title. In : Journal. vol. Volume, Date, pp. Page.

will format records of type paper, placing author field first followed by a period, the article title follows ended by a period which is in turn followed by the word 'In :', and the journal title, a period, volume of the journal preceded by the word 'vol.', date of publication preceded by a comma and followed by a comma which is again followed by the word 'pp.' and the actual pagination. A sample output will thus look like:

Chowdhury, G.G. Natural language processing and information retrieval: basic issues. In: IASLIC Bulletin. vol. 36, 1991, pp. 45-49.

7.9 SUMMARY

This chapter describes the various steps that one has to follow for developing a database using a text retrieval software, citing examples from Micro-CDS/ISIS and ideaList. It may be noted that the specific steps and measures prescribed for each operation differ from software to software. However, some points may be generalised.

The first step obviously relates to an understanding of the functionality of the proposed system. Once this is ascertained, that is, the functions to be performed by the system are known, the next questions relate to the nature and number of documents to be incorporated into the database, and the nature and number of target users. These information help the designer in his tasks.

With these basic considerations, one has to follow the specific prescriptions of the chosen software. The major tasks involved here are:

1. Designing the structure of the database;
2. Decisions regarding the generation of the index file;
3. Decisions regarding the format for display of data;
4. Designing the worksheet or form for data entry;
5. Creation of records;
6. Generation of index file;
7. Searching the database; and
8. Displaying, sorting, and printing of records.

Some text retrieval systems have certain in-built facilities for performing some of the abovementioned tasks, and therefore they need not be performed by the user (designer). For example, we have seen that steps 3, 4, and 6 mentioned above are automatically performed in the ideaList software.

One important step, not discussed above, is monitoring the performance of the system. This is important because a text retrieval system may not perform the desired functions at a given stage, or one may want to improve the performance of the system to a certain level. This calls for close observation of the performance of the system, and finding out the reasons for failure, if any. Thus, factors for improvements may be noted down for necessary modification at one or more stages of the system.

REFERENCES

1. R. Ardern and C. Hamilton. Systems for text retrieval : the hardware and software environment. In: I. Rowlands, ed. Text Retrieval: an Introduction. London, Taylor Graham, 1987, pp. 27-49.
2. S. N. Sur and G.G. Chowdhury. A Prototype Design of a Bibliographic Database based on CCF using Micro-CDS/ ISIS. *Iaslic Bulletin*, 38 ( ), 1993.
3. A. Di Lauro. *IDIN Manual: for the Creation and Management of a Bibliographic Database Using Micro-CDS/ISIS.* Paris, OECD, 1988.
4. A. Di Lauro. *Manual for Preparing Records in Microcomputer-based Bibliographic Information Systems.* Canada, IDRC,

1990 (IDRC-TS67e).
5. *CDS/ISIS Manual (version 2.3)*, UNESCO, Paris, 1989.
6. ideaList MS-DOS. Oct. 1991 version. Oxford, Blackwell Scientific Publications, 1991.
7. S. Stigleman. ideaList: Flexible Text Storage and Retrieval Software. *Database*, June 1992, 50-56.

Chapter 8
Overview of Selected Text Retrieval Packages

8.1 INTRODUCTION

Major text retrieval software were initially developed to work on mainframe or minicomputers. Gradually with the availability of more powerful computers some companies began to bring out microversions of their software products. Quite a number of software packages are now available which are solely designed to work in micro computer environment. Several attempts have been made over the past few years to evaluate these text retrieval packages[1-6]. These evaluations have, for justifiable reasons, limited their studies to some selected packages. This chapter presents an overview of six selected text retrieval packages preceded by a brief introduction to some evaluation studies of text retrieval software reported in literature.

8.2 SOME EVALUATION STUDIES

Rowley[2, 7] mentions that one of the most difficult aspects of reviewing the available text retrieval software relates to the choice of packages. There are two general approaches. One approach which has been taken in the IIS directory[5] is to define packages as text retrieval packages if their suppliers or producers view those as suitable for text retrieval operations. Another approach is to identify the features which are typical of text retrieval software and to select packages which more or less satisfy those requirements.

Ashford[1] in his evaluation study with nine packages, *viz.*, ADP/3RIP, ASSASSIN6, BASIS, CAIRS, DECO, DOCU/MASTER, INFOText, SEARCH, and STATUS, identified that all the systems share a number of features. Following are the features which Ashford[1] found available in all the packages:

1. Boolean query formulation
2. Search refinements
3. Field/Section limit on search
4. File/Chapter limit on search
5. Display of 'postings' frequencies
6. Truncation
7. Text string searching
8. Stored searches or stored questions
9. Stopword list
10. Synonym recognition
11. Vocabulary control
12. Help facilities
13. Sorting of search results
14. Editing of search results
15. Formatting of output
16. Database security

Rowley[3] mentions that in addition to these basic features some mainframe and minicomputer versions of text retrieval software offer some additional features like

1. Different forms of user dialogue
2. Current awareness services
3. Word processing
4. Statistical analysis facilities
5. Display of index
6. Subject index generation
7. Electronic mail
8. Report generation
9. Left truncation
10. Right truncation
11. Middle truncation
12. Character masking (wild card)
13. Long record features, *etc.*

Deciding the criteria for a comparative study is as difficult as choosing the packages for evaluation. The Free Text Retrieval Working Party of the Inter-University Software Committee (IUSC) in UK,[8] identified eight broad categories of functions which are supposed to be provided by a good free text retrieval software, *viz.*

1. definition and re-definition of text structures and contents;

2. retrieval of documents and document sets;
3. formatting the output of retrieved documents;
4. control and analysis of document terminology;
5. addition, deletion and modification of documents;
6. recovery from software and hardware failures;
7. control of access to data and facilities dependent on the status of the inquirer; and
8. monitoring of database use and performance.

The IIS directory[5], which provides a comparative study of 100 text retrieval software, have chosen the following points for comparison:

1. Market features
   a. Price
   b. Maintenance
   c. Number
   d. Number of years in UK market
2. Programming languages
3. System features
   a. Maximum number of users
   b. Maximum record size
4. Indexing
   a. Gowords
   b. Stopwords
   c. Multiword terms
   d. Thesaurus
5. Information retrieval features
   a. Boolean query formulation
   b. Nesting (Bracketing)
   c. Proximity searching
   d. Field searching
   e. Search refinements
   f. Truncation—left, right, internal character masking (wild card)
   g. Range searching
   h. Browse on index
   i. Text string searching
6. Output
   a. SDI
   b. User-defined output formats
   c. Menu-based interface

   d. Command-based interface
7. Security
   a. Passwords
   b. User ID
   c. Data encryption
   d. Various levels of security
8. Interfaces and integrated modules
   a. Downloading software
   b. Electronic mail software
   c. Graphics software
   d. Image processing software
   e. Spreadsheet software
   f. Accounting software
   g. Financial modelling software
   h. Word processing software
   i. Videotex
   j. Acquisitions
   k. Circulation control
   l. Cataloguing
   m. OPAC
   n. General DBMS
   o. CD-ROM
   p. Chemical structure software
9. Contract
   a. Help desk
   b. Manuals
   c. On-site training
   d. Off-site training
   e. Consultancy
   f. User group

8.3 CHOSEN PACKAGES FOR EVALUATION

Six text retrieval packages have been chosen here to present an overview. The objective here is not to provide exclusive comparative figures, but to present a broad overview of the packages. For detailed features of these packages readers may consult available published sources[4-6] and concerned manuals. The packages chosen for this overview run in microcomputer environments, though they are also available in mainframe and/or minicomputer versions.

The chosen packages are—BASIS (PC version), BRS/Search (C version), CAIRS (micro version), CDS/ISIS (micro version), ideaList, and STATUS (PC version). The following points have been considered to study the chosen software packages:

1. Basic information features relating to
   a. supplier;
   b. hardware requirements;
   c. programming language;
   d. price, *etc.*
2. Input/output facilities which include
   a. data input, editing;
   b. system restrictions;
   c. user-defined output, *etc.*
3. Indexing facilities which include
   a. Use of stopwords list;
   b. Use of thesaurus;
   c. Multi-word indexing;
   d. Index display;
4. Search facilities including the provisions for
   a. Boolean searching;
   b. Nested Boolean searching;
   c. Search refinement;
   d. Proximity searching;
   e. Field searching;
   f. Left truncation;
   g. Right truncation;
   h. Wild truncation;
   i. Range search;
   j. Text string searching.

8.4 BASIC FEATURES OF THE CHOSEN PACKAGES

Micro-CDS/ISIS is available from UNESCO or any of its distribution centres in the member countries. It is written in Pascal and runs on IBM PC, PC-XT, PC-AT IBM PC compatibles, and WANG PC, with at least 512KB RAM. CDS/ISIS is either provided free of charge or with a very nominal price to non-profit organisations.

BRS/Search has been developed by BRS Information Technologies. It can run on UNIX Micros, XENIX Micros,

VMS Micros, VM/CMS Micros, and MS-DOS Micros with 512KB RAM. It is written in C. Price ranges from US $ 1,000 onwards.[5]

Micro-CAIRS is produced by Leatherhead Food Research Association, Surrey, UK. It is written in Assembler and RTL. The system needs a minimum of 256KB RAM and runs on IBM PC, IBM PS/2, IBM compatibles WANG PC, *etc.* Micro-CAIRS is available in three versions, viz. Micro-CAIRS IMS, Micro-CAIRS LMS, and Micro-CAIRS TMS. Price varies in different versions and ranges from £ 600 to 2,800.[5]

BASIS is available from Information Dimensions Inc., Dublin. It is written in a combination of FORTRAN and Assembler language and runs on DEC Micro VAX. Price of this package is about the same as BRS/Search.[5]

STATUS is available from CP International, New York. It is written in FORTRAN. It needs minimum 512KB RAM and runs on IBM PC and IBM PC compatibles. Price of this package is £ 1,500.[5]

ideaList has been produced recently by the Blackwell Scientific Publications, Oxford. It needs 512KB RAM and runs on IBM PC and IBM PC compatibles. Price of this package is US $ 225 for single-user version and US $ 595 for a five-user network version.[9]

8.5 INPUT/OUTPUT FACILITIES OF THE CHOSEN PACKAGES

A text retrieval package should provide interactive data input and editing facilities. Almost all the text retrieval packages available nowadays provide these facilities. In each case data can be input via online and batch mode. They also provide facilities of online data editing.

The packages under study vary in terms of their system restrictions. While ideaList restricts maximum number of records to 32,750, in other packages number of records is normally limited by the size of the hard disk; in BRS/Search and CDS/ISIS maximum number of records could go as high as 16 millions.

One important feature of CDS/ISIS is that user can specify the format in which data will be displayed. However, in all the packages users can specify a particular format in which output can be printed.

8.6 INDEXING FACILITIES OF THE CHOSEN PACKAGES

One of the most common features of text retrieval packages is to have index terms stored in inverted file. In some packages, only one inverted file is created for all index terms, while in some multiple indices are created. In some text retrieval packages index entries are created automatically for all the terms those occur in the records, while in others user can specify which terms will be indexed and thus can avoid wasting storage space and other problems of maintaining a large index file. Unwanted terms can also be dropped from the index by creating a list of stopwords; almost all text retrieval packages provide facilities for creating stopword lists.

CDS/ISIS uses a single inverted file for each and every database, which functions as multiple indices. The most important feature is that one can identify the searchable fields for each database through Field Select Table (FST). An optional file called *Any File*, associated with the inverted file, can be created; terms included in the Any file allows to conduct 'blanket searching'. CDS/ISIS allows to create stopwords file which contains the list of non-significant words; it also allows to build up a thesaurus. Eight kinds of *Indexing Techniques*, each of which specifies a particular process for data extraction, are available in CDS/ISIS. The *Terms Dictionary* can be displayed on the screen. Searchers can use their own thesaurus.

In BRS/Search index entries are automatically generated for each word in input documents; inverted file may be divided into three smaller files in order to improve disk access and response time for large databases. Users can specify stopword list. Indexes are browsable. BRS/ Search allows to build up a thesaurus.

In BASIS index entries are automatically generated for each word in input documents or for the contents of designated fields and subfields. Unique index entries can be created by concatenating designated field values. Users can specify stopword list. Indexes are browsable.

Micro-CAIRS offers a choice of indexing methodologies which can be utilised alone or in combination. CAIRS can also generate automatic index entries for each word in all or specified fields. There is an optional thesaurus which can be used for data entry and retrieval. A stopword list can be created to eliminate non-significant words.

In STATUS index entries are automatically generated for each word; users can specify stopword list. Indexes are automatically modified when new records are added to a database.

In ideaList index entries are automatically generated for each word; user can create stopword list for non-significant words. Synonyms can be stored in a text file. Index terms can be displayed.

8.7 SEARCH FACILITIES OF THE CHOSEN PACKAGES

Text retrieval packages are usually characterised by wide ranging search facilities. The packages under study provide a number of sophisticated search options, the most significant ones are described in the following sections.

8.7.1 Boolean Operators

Boolean operators (AND, OR, NOT) are used to combine more than one search terms in a search expression. All the chosen packages allow to link multiple search terms with Boolean operators. In addition, STATUS, CDS/ISIS and CAIRS allow nesting of search terms. In all the packages Boolean AND, OR, NOT operators can be used to link multiple search terms or previously established sets of retrieved records.

It may be noted that the notations used to represent Boolean operators vary from software to software. Following are some of the examples:

ideaList

pigeon OR parrot
(will retrieve records where either of the terms occurs)

BRS/Search

computer AND information
(will retrieve records where both the terms occur)

computer OR information
(will retrieve records where either of the terms occurs)
computer NOT information
(will retrieve records where the first term occurs, but not the second)

CDS/ISIS

computer * information
(will retrieve records where both the terms occur)
computer + information
(will retrieve records where either of the terms occurs)

STATUS

computer + information?
(will retrieve records where both the search terms occur)
computer, information?
(will retrieve records where either of the terms occurs)

8.7.2 Search Refinement

If the output of a given search does not fulfil the requirement of a user, he/she can call the previous search expression and can edit the search expression as necessary. This is called search refinement and it supports narrowing or broadening of the previous search in order to arrive at a better result. All the chosen packages have the search refinement facility.

8.7.3 Proximity Searching

Proximity or adjacency searching allows the searcher to retrieve items having occurrence of more than one search terms within a specified number of terms. In other words, the searcher can specify the number of terms those may occur within two search terms; this may be limited to the same line, same sentence, same paragraph, *etc.*, of a given record.

BASIS allows proximity searches to retrieve documents containing search terms located within a specified number of words of one another. Users can specify the sequence of terms for proximity searches.

In Micro-CAIRS Proximity searches can retrieve documents containing search terms located within a specified number of words of one another.

In STATUS Proximity searches can retrieve documents containing search terms located in an exact distance from one another or within a specified number of words of one another. Users can specify the sequence of terms for proximity searches. Proximity searches can be limited to the same paragraph.

BRS/Search allows Proximity searches to retrieve documents containing search terms located in the same paragraph, in the same sentence, or within a specified number of words of one another. Users can specify the sequence of terms for proximity searches.

In CDS/ISIS Proximity searches can retrieve documents containing terms located in the same field, individual occurrence of a repeatable field, or within a specified number of words, or exactly a specified number of words.

In ideaList Proximity searches can retrieve adjacent search terms, thereby supporting phrase searches. One special search feature of ideaList is *sound-alike searching*, which retrieves all the words those sound similar, *e.g.*, 'SMITH', 'SMITHE', *etc.*

Following are some of the examples of proximity searches in the chosen packages:

CDS/ISIS

information $ management
(will retrieve those records where the term 'information' and 'management' occur adjacent to each other)

information $$ management
(will retrieve those records where one word occurs between the two search terms)

microcomputer (F) library
(will retrieve those records where both the search terms occur in the same field)

BASIS

SCAN field information w<4 management

(will retrieve those records where the search terms are separated by upto four terms)
SCAN field information ADJ management
(will retrieve those records where the term 'information' occurs adjacent to 'management')

BRS/Search

information ADJ management
(will retrieve those records where the term 'information' occurs adjacent to 'management')
information WITH management
(will retrieve those records where the search terms occur in the same sentence)
information NEAR management
(will retrieve those records where 'information' is followed by 'management' or vice versa)
SET NEARLEVEL = 3
information NEAR management
(will retrieve those documents where 'information' occurs within three words of 'management')

STATUS

information management?
(will retrieve those records where the term 'information' directly precedes 'management')
information/1,999/management?
(will retrieve those records where 'information' precedes 'management' in the same paragraph)

8.7.4 Field Searching

One can specify a particular field to be searched by the search terms with the particular field name or field number. This is usually done to restrict a search within one or more specified fields and also to avoid false drops that may result due to the occurrence of the search term in the undesired field(s). For example, a user may want to retrieve all those items where the term 'Calcutta' occurs in the 'title' field, but not in the 'imprint' field; in the former case the search term is related to the content of the document whereas in the latter it denotes place of publication. All the packages under consideration provide facilities for limiting a search in one or more fields. Following are some of the examples of field searching in the chosen packages:

CDS/ISIS

Computer + communication /(4)
(will retrieve those records where either of the search terms occurs in field, identified by tag 4)

ideaList

author = harris
(will retrieve all those records the search term 'harris' occurs in the 'author' field)

BRS/Search

bird.PET.
(will retrieve all those records where the search term 'bird' occurs in the 'pet' field)

STATUS

(computer + information) @ TITLE?
(will retrieve all those records where both the search term occur in the 'title' field)

8.7.5 Truncation

Truncation of search term is a facility by which a user can conduct one search for all those terms which have some part in common rather than conducting separate search for each term. There are different kinds of truncation which can be applied to search for terms having the root in common (right truncation), the end or the suffix in common (left truncation), both the prefix and suffix in common (middle truncation), etc. In addition, there is another kind of truncation called the wild truncation by which a user can retrieve all those items which have some posting in a given field, no matter what the term is. All the packages support right truncation for root word searches whereas BASIS, BRS/Search, ideaList and Micro-CAIRS support left truncation for suffix searches. IdeaList and BRS/Search support middle truncation. BASIS, Micro-CAIRS, STATUS, ideaList, and CDS/ISIS support wild card (truncation).

Following are some examples of truncated search expressions from the chosen packages:

ideaList

computer*
(will retrieve records having the terms 'computer', 'computers', 'computerisation', *etc.*)
*hyl
(will retrieve records having the terms 'methyl', 'ethyl', *etc.*)

BRS/Search

computer $
(will retrieve records having the term 'computer', 'computers', 'computerisation', *etc.*)
$fish
(will retrieve records having terms ending with 'fish', e.g., 'selfish')
$fish$
(will retrieve records having the term 'fish' embedded within, *e.g.*, 'selfishness')
b$ush
(will retrieve records with an embedded character string after b and before 'ush', *e.g.*, 'blush')

CDS/ISIS

computer*
(will retrieve records with terms having the same common root 'computer', *e.g.*, 'computer', 'computers', 'computerization', *etc.*)

STATUS

computer*?
(will retrieve records having terms with the same common root 'computer')

8.7.6 Range Search

Range search facilitates retrieval of items whose key value lies within the range given in the search expression, for example, all books published between 1990-1992. This facility is usually used to search for numeric values. Relational operators like greater than, less than, equals, *etc.*, are used in isolation or in combination in range searching. All the packages under consideration allow range searching on numerical data and date.

8.7.7 String Search

One of the characteristic features of text retrieval packages is the provision for string searching. String search facilitates retrieval of records having the search term which is not included in the inverted file; this is obviously a relatively slow process for a large database, and therefore is useful in such a case where a small subset has already been retrieved by an inverted file search. All the packages but ideaList provide string search facility. In addition to the normal inverted file searching, CDS/ISIS provides a facility for *Free Text Searching* which allows users to search text strings those do not occur in the inverted file.

8.8 SUMMARY

This study shows that all the chosen packages provide more or less similar facilities for data input, output and search. Therefore, the ultimate choice should be based on the local needs and capabilities. However, price is an important factor, and in this respect weightage goes towards CDS/ISIS. It may be noted that CDS/ISIS is the only package available free of charge. There are other advantageous features of CDS/ISIS too. It allows 16 millions records in a database; it runs on a wide range of micros from IBM PC/XTs. However, CDS/ISIS has also got certain limitations like lack of online help facilities, unfriendly user interface, etc., which are discussed in Chapter 10 of this book. Among other packages, ideaList is the cheapest though it is suitable only for small libraries, because it can manage only a few thousand records.

To meet the requirements of all kinds of users, microcomputer-based text retrieval packages should run on Local Area Network (LAN) to allow more than one users to have access to a given database at a time. CDS/ISIS runs on LAN. Version 2.33 of CDS/ISIS can be mounted on a LAN, as was done in the Department of Information Studies, University of Sheffield using the Novell Netware

System.[10] However, versions 3.0 onwards of CDS/ISIS, are the formal network versions. Network versions of software are usually dearer in comparison to stand-alone versions. The network version of ideaList is however quite cheap.

Ideally, text retrieval packages should have flexibility to adapt to the local needs, which means that users should have a choice to extend the existing facilities of the package to suit the special needs. This is rarely available from commercial packages. One distinguishing features of CDS/ISIS is its Advanced Programming Facilities which can be used to develop application programs (or utilities) to meet specific purposes. Some attempts have been made to develop systems for various library management operations using the CDS/ISIS Pascal. interface. These are discussed in Chapter 10 of this book.

REFERENCES

1. J. Ashford, Storage and Retrieval of Bibliographic Records: a Comparison of Database Management System (DBMS) and Free Text Approaches, *Program*, Vol. 19, No. 1, 1984, 16-45.
2. J. Rowley, An Overview of the Available Text Retrieval Software. In: Text Retrieval in Context: Proceedings of the Institute of Information Scientists Text Retrieval '84 Conference, ed. by R. Kimberley, London, Taylor Graham, 1985, 46-60.
3. J. Rowley, Text Retrieval Software 1985: a Survey of Recent Developments. In: Integrating Text With Non-text—a Picture is Worth 1K Words: Proceedings of the Institute of Information Scientists Text Retrieval '85 Conference, ed. by R. Kimberley, London, Taylor Graham, 1986, 19-35.
4. W. Saffady, *Text Storage and Retrieval Systems: a Technology Survey and Product Directory*, London, Meckler, 1989.
5. R. Kimberley, ed. *Text Retrieval: a Directory of Software*, ed. 3, Aldershot, Gower, 1990.
6. H. Dyer and A. Gunson, eds. *A Directory of Library and Information Retrieval Software for Microcomputers*, Ed. 4, Aldershot, Gower, 1990.
7. J. Rowley, What is Text Retrieval and Why is it Important. In: Text Retrieval: an Introduction, ed. by I. Rowlands, London, Taylor Graham, 1987, 1-13.
8. M. Bain *et. al.*, *Free Text Retrieval Systems: A Review and*

Evaluation. London, Taylor Graham, 1989.

9. S. Stigleman, ideaList: Flexible Text Storage and Retrieval Software. *Database*, June 1992, 50-56.
10. S. Chowdhury and G.G. Chowdhury. Text Retrieval Systems: an Overview. In: A. Chatterjee, S.K. Sen and S.K. Kapoor, eds. Information Retrieval: Models and Techniques, Papers, XV National Seminar of IASLIC, Annamalai University, Annamalainagar (Tamil Nadu), 26-29 Dec. 1992, pp. 35-41.

Chapter 9
Text Retrieval, DBMS and Library Management Systems

9.1 INTRODUCTION

It has been noted in Chapter 4 and Chapter 5 that text retrieval packages specialise in handling variable length fields and textual data where the required retrieval or search key is not predictable. Access to records in such databases is usually through an inverted file, and a wide range of retrieval facilities can be expected. Database Management Systems (DBMS), on the other hand, are designed to support the creation of databases for a variety of different applications; they are capable of handling related databases, and are essentially programming frameworks which can be used to create a database application. This chapter addresses the basic differences between text retrieval and database management systems and discusses another kind of system—library management system.

Ideally speaking, a suitable system for performing all library operations and services should include facilities of both the text retrieval and database management operations. Such systems are called library management systems. These systems are usually created on a relational database management framework which allows them to handle more than one related data file that are particularly useful for a number of library housekeeping operations. These systems also provide some text retrieval features with particular reference to OPAC facilities.

9.2 DBMS VS. TEXT RETRIEVAL

In a conventional database management environment, a given database comprises different records each having specific information incorporated in a field. Thus, the information or attribute contained in any field is unique to characterise the given record. In a database of employees, each record may contain specific information about a given employee, *e.g.*, his/her name, address, age, salary, job classification, *etc.*, and each attribute value pertains unequivocally to the corresponding employee record. In retrieval of information from the database, a given query is expected to match with a given field value, *e.g.*, employee name, and if the query matches exactly with the database information, then and only then retrieval takes place. Thus, the two major characterising features of database management systems are

— each item of information provided in a given field can uniquely represent the particular attribute of that record, and

— retrieval takes place only when there is a perfect match between the query and the database information.

In a bibliographic information retrieval environment, the retrieval activity can be conceptually similar to the search and retrieval of database records.[1] In a bibliographic database, each record represents a given bibliographic item (book, periodical article, *etc.*), the different fields of which provide unique information about the given item like author, title, publisher, date of publication, *etc.* Thus the attribute of each field in a bibliographic record is conceptually similar to that of a conventional database and consequently searching and retrieval can take place in the similar way. There is, however, a major difference which arises in case of retrieval of information through subject approach. In a bibliographic retrieval system, each text (document) is represented by a few content identifiers or keywords. Thus in a given field there may be a number of keywords each of which represents or characterises the given text partially. Because text retrieval or information retrieval operations depend directly on the content representations used to describe the stored records, a substantial amount of time and energy is to be devoted for analysing the content of stored texts. In a database management environment the question of content analysis and representation does not arise.

The second difference between text retrieval and database management systems arises out of retrieval matching. In a text retrieval environment, retrieval takes place even when there is a partial match between the query and the stored information. This does not happen in a database management environment; retrieval takes place only when there is an exact match.

In a text retrieval environment, a given search statement may comprise a number of content identifiers which need to be ordered in a logical way to create the best possible query. This often is a complex task, and users need to be provided sufficient guidelines for the purpose. In a database management environment, queries usually concern with a particular value (or sometimes a range, *e.g.*, managers with a salary between one to two hundred thousands and aged between 40 to 45), and therefore formulation of a query is relatively easier which has further been simplified with the provision of QBE (Query By Example) in database management software.

Thus some of the major differences between text retrieval and database management systems can be represented as—

1. A DBMS is designed to deal with 'structured' data whereas a text retrieval system is supposed to deal with 'unstructured' data.
2. In a DBMS user's information needs are exact and the matching criterion for retrieval is also exact, but in a text retrieval environment user's information needs are often vague and partial matching is also accepted.
3. Text retrieval systems usually support an essentially fixed application, *viz.*, 'storage and retrieval of data objects of a type', with selection conditions, *etc.*, parameterised. DBMSs usually supply an infrastructure for a variety of applications defined by the user in the areas of file management and multi-user support.
4. Text retrieval systems access what is really only a

single record type, but DBMSs are much concerned with cross-linking between different record types.
5. Text retrieval systems assume a relatively static collection of data with occasional mass addition, whereas DBMSs are often involved with online updating with transaction concurrence.

However, as Rowley[2] mentions, the boundaries between text retrieval and database management systems have been eroded over the past few years and it is often difficult to draw clear-cut distinctions between the two categories of systems.

9.3 LIBRARY MANAGEMENT SYSTEMS

Broadly speaking, library management systems encompass all those automated systems which a library runs in order to manage and control its collection. Library management operations include all the internal housekeeping operations that the library adopts to handle the selection, ordering, cataloguing, and the lending of library materials.[3]

Library management systems are designed to automate cataloguing (conventional information retrieval) and housekeeping operations in libraries. In order to understand the main features of library management software, one has to understand the requirements for each house-keeping operation, the nature of data handled, and so on. The basic requirements for four major house-keeping activities performed in libraries are discussed in the following sections.

9.3.1 Acquisition

The functions and procedures carried out as part of an acquisition system are as follows:

1. Items are checked before ordering in order to avoid duplication.
2. A file of budget allocation is maintained which is to be consulted before placing an order.
3. A file of items-on-order is maintained.
4. Orders are processed.
5. Chasers are produced for overdue items.

6. Receipt is recorded with details of price and invoice.
7. Accession numbers are allocated.
8. Record of fund is maintained.

To cope with these routines, one would require an acquisition system to be able to format and print records in a variety of ways and according to a number of selection criteria depending on whether one wanted to generate order letter, urgent order letter, overdue reminders, cancellation letter, and so on. These requirements call for a retrieval system along with a report generator. Other requirements call for formal database management approach. Such requirements are as follows:

— easy input of supplier details usually by supplier code, and a link among the bibliographic file (catalogue), order file and supplier file is required;
— budget and accounting control procedures access a file of fund codes and expenditure and update these automatically;
— from time to time order file is checked to locate overdue items for which reminders are to be issued;
— generation of different kinds of statistics, *e.g.*, money spent by a given or all departments over a period of time, amount committed, amount left for further purchase, performance of an individual vendor, and so on.

All these activities are to be carried out online and in real time. The library manager should be able to find out instantly items on order, items overdue, funds exhausted, funds committed, and so on.

9.3.2 Circulation

Circulation control system includes a number of activities, *viz.*, issue and return of items, reservation of items, issue of overdue reminders, recall notices, *etc.* A circulation control system is required to record:

1. Details of items on loan.
2. Details of borrowers.
3. Date of issue and due date for each item that has been lent out.

4. Reservation details, *etc.*

In order to perform circulation activities, data elements which are required are:

— record for each item in the library's stock;
— record for each borrower including borrower status, loan limit, and so on;
— material or category codes to implement loan policy, length of time for which a given item can be lent, *etc.*;
— fields for entering information relating to date of issue and date of return of items;
— records must include "reserved" status flag and links to reservation details.

Thus the system is expected to maintain a file of the library materials along with the current status of each item, *i.e.*, on loan or not, if on loan then to whom and when issued, when due for return, etc. The system should also maintain link with the borrower file for online enquiry about issue and for production of notices. There will be a constant change in the data—each transaction calls for an update in different database, for example, the main collection or catalogue database, borrower database, loan and reservation database, and so on. These updates should be made automatically. The system should be able to produce overdue notices, emergency recall notices, and various statistics relating to issue, return, *etc.*

9.3.3 Serials Control

Serials control is a complex task in libraries. It involves a number of activities which include:

1. Maintaining a list of journal titles being subscribed.
2. Controlling subscriptions.
3. Keeping track of renewal dates.
4. Controlling funds for purchase of journals.
5. Recording the receipts of each part of journals.
6. Identifying and claiming missing or overdue issues.
7. Distributing issues to target users.

Therefore, a serials control system should maintain the details of

— titles and holdings;

— dates for renewal of each subscription;
— cost of subscription and appropriate fund codes;
— frequency codes and dates of receipt of each issue;
— details of suppliers/agents; and
— names of borrowers on circulation lists.

In terms of system functions, a serials control system requires

— regular updates of files;
— speedy entry of receipt of issues with prompt recognition of anomalies, if any, for example missing parts;
— ability to print distribution lists for each issue as received; and
— ability to generate instantly various statistical reports.

9.3.4 Online Catalogue

The least complex house-keeping operation is maintaining online catalogue. Some people recognise this as part of information retrieval operations rather than house-keeping operations. However, a library has to create a bibliographic database with required data items through which users are expected to conduct their search. An on-line public access catalogue should, along with the normal considerations for creating a bibliographic database, consider factors like data exchange format, factors relating to network, resource-sharing, *etc.*

9.4 SOFTWARE FOR LIBRARY MANAGEMENT

Origin of automated library systems date back to 1960s. During the early sixties, several libraries in the USA and UK began to experiment with the possibilities of using computer in various library and information related activities. While dealing with different aspects of automation, several standards for bibliographic description and format were developed during the mid and late- sixties.

During the early seventies many libraries began to use their parent body's computer systems to develop local information systems. These systems were custom-built by the in-house or specifically appointed computer professionals. However, the situation soon started changing, and different companies came forward to build software for various library and infromation-oriented activities.

Seventies also saw a growth of activities in achieving library cooperation and resource-sharing. By about mid-seventies, online search services were available in some big libraries. The development of off-the-shelf software packages for library automation was significant during the late seventies and eighties. The early systems were meant for main-frame computers, and later each company started bringing out minicomputer versions of their software, because from late seventies libraries began to install minicomputer systems specifically charged with library automation activities.

However, due to sharp growth in the microcomputer world during the mid- and late-eighties, several microcomputer-based software for handling library and information activities were developed. Many of these software are again capable of running on a local area network, thereby providing a cheap offer for automation environment to libraries.

Today there is a large number of companies throughout the world engaged in providing systems for library management purposes. There have been several guides and publications relating to library management software.[4-6] In the latest edition of her book, Tedd[7] provides brief information relating to 23 library management software. Larsen[8] mentions that more than 1,300 large integrated library management systems and more than 3,600 small integrated library management systems have been installed in the 12 European Community (EC) countries. Larsen[8] also provides twenty mostly used large and small integrated library management packages in the 12 EC countries. These are listed in Tables 9.1 and 9.2 along with the names of their producers/suppliers as a means of providing some examples.

Table 9.1: Top 20 Library Management Systems in the EC Countries (Larsen[8])

Software	*Supplier, Country*
Adlib	Databasix, UK
Aleph	Ex Libraries, Israel
BIBDIA	Nord Partner, Norway
BIS	DABIS, Germany
BLS	BLCMP, UK
DOBIS/LIBIS	IBM, USA
Dynix	Dynix, USA
GALAXY	DS Ltd., USA
GLIS	Geac, Canada
LIBER	LIBER, France
LIBERTAS	SLS, UK
LIBS/100	CLSI, USA
OPSYS	OPSYS, France
RC-LIB	ICL Data, Denmark
SBN	3 Software Houses, Italy
SISIS	Siemens AG, Germnay
Supermax	DDE, Denmark
TOBIAS	Datapoint, France
URICA	McDonnel Douglas, USA
VUBIS	CEVI, Belgium

Several software for handling library management operations have also come out in India during the last few years. At least 20 such software packages have come to the notice of the present author. Table 9.3 provides a list of these software packages.

Table 9.2: Top 20 Small Library Management Systems in the EC Countries (Larsen[8])

Software	*Supplier, Country*
BIBSIS	Lou G. Mom, Netherlands
BIBLIOMATIK	Dantek, Denmark
BIS-LOK	DABIS, Germany
Bookshe1F	SCSS, UK
BookshelF PC	Logical Choice, UK
CAIRS-LMS	Leatherhead Food RA, UK
CALM	Pyramid Computer, UK
CD DIGEST	Softnet, Portugal
dLIB	D.R.F. vanBreman, Netherlands
DOLPHIN	Dolphin, UK
LARS	WEKA Software Fur and Wirtschaft und, Verwaltung, Germany
LIBRARIAN	Eurotec Consultants, UK
LIBRARY PAC	Information Systems Design, UK
MICRO-LIBRARY SYSTEM	Top Technology, UK
MICRO-LIBRARIAN	Micro Library Professional, UK
OASIS	Dawson Technology, UK
OCELOT	Various (in NL and BE), Canada
Soutron	Soutron Ltd., UK
TINlib	IME, UK
UNIBIBLIO	Copin, Italy

We have already seen that text retrieval systems deal with stored text and provide multiple access points to users, provide sophisticated search facilities, and allow to format the retrieved output in a desired way. Thus infromation retrieval purposes in libraries are met by these systems. However, text retrieval systems are designed to deal with one database at a time while library management operations require handling of more than one files (databases) at a time. For example, an acquisition system requires handling of book file, supplier file, fund file, order file, *etc.*, However, commercial producers of text retrieval systems have long been engaged in providing some means with their packages with which those can be adopted to library housekeeping operations.

Table 9.3 List of Software of Indian Origin For Handling Library Related Activities

Software	*Source*
Archives (1,2,3)	Microfax Electronic Systems, Bombay
ACQUAS, ASCAT, ASCIR ASIRE, SERAS	Ober Information System, Calcutta
Catman	INSDOC, New Delhi
Golden LIBRA	Golden Age Software Technologies, Bombay
LIBRARIAN (2.1 and 3.1)	Soft-Aid, Pune
Library Management	Raychan Sysmatics, Bangalore
Library Manager	System Data Control Pvt. Ltd. Bombay
LibSoft	ET & T Corpn., New Delhi
LibSys, Micro-LibSys	LibSys Corpn., New Delhi
Listplus	Computer Systems, Bangalore
LoanSoft	Computek Computer Systems, Hyderabad
MAITRAYEE	(Developed by) CMC, Calcutta (for the CALIBNET Project)
MECSYS	MECON, Ranchi
NILIS	Asmita Consultants, Bombay
NIRMALS	Nirmal Institute of Computer Expertise, Tiruchirapalli
SALIM	Uptron India Ltd., New Delhi
SANJAY	(Developed by) DESIDOC, New Delhi (Under a NISSAT Project)
Slim 1.1	Algorythms, Bombay
TULIPS	Tata Unisys Ltd., Bombay
WILISYS	Wipro India, Bangalore

9.5 LIBRARY MANAGEMENT AND TEXT RETRIEVAL SYSTMS

Library management systems like BLCMP, Geac, *etc.*, provide text retrieval facilities along with the modules for different housekeeping operations. All library management systems include facilities for OPAC (Online Public Access Catalogue) which meet the users' infromation retrieval requirements.

Many text retrieval packages provide specific, often optional, modules for housekeeping operations. Packages like ADLIB2, BOOKSHELFPC, LIBRA, TINlib, *etc.*, provide integrated library housekeeping system. Similarly, some packages provide module(s) for one or more library management operations. For example, ADLIB2, MICROCAIRS-LMS, TINlib, *etc.* provide modules for serials control; TINlib provides module for interlibrary loan; ADLIB2, LIBRA, MICROCAIRS-LMS, TINlib, *etc.*, provide modules for issue system; ADLIB2, BOOKSHELFPC, LIBRA, TINlib, *etc.*, provide modules for acquisitions, and so on.

Out of the six text retrieval packages studied in Chapter 7, four systems provide additional modules or interfacing facilities for a number of house-keeping operations. While ideaList does not make any provision for any library house-keeping operations, one can develop new modules (application programs) for various library management operations using the Pascal interface provided with the CDS/ISIS software. This is one of the unique features of CDS/ISIS. Attempts have already been made to develop library management software using this facility.[9-11]

The software developed for the CALIBNET (Calcutta Library Network) is an example of a library management software developed in India that has been developed on the top of INGRES.[12] This package, when marketed, will support normal library management operations like cataloguing, acquisition, circulation control, serials control, union catalogue management, and so on. It will also provide facilities for library networking; the communication software uses TCP/IP with X.25 protocol for networking. These packages along with a few other software packages developed in India for handling text retrieval and library management operations are discussed in Chapter 10 of this book.

9.6 TREND IN THE DEVELOPMENT OF LIBRARY MANAGEMENT SYSTEMS

Tedd[7] mentions that the trend during eighties was that larger libraries moved from a shared to stand-alone services, perhaps with a link to a central shared database of bibliographic records. However, there have been significant changes due to the appearance of more powerful microcomputer-based packages during the last few years. These packages run on a local area network and provide libraries an alternative, and perhaps cheaper solution to library automation.

Looking at the library systems prevailing in the European market, Larsen[8] noted the following trends in the development of library management software:

1. Product differentiation is beginning to narrow down rapidly; all the packages are capable of performing almost all the necessary functions.
2. The OPAC interface needs some enhancements, like inclusion of intelligent user interface, capability of accepting natural language queries, and so on.
3. Few systems offer facilities for integretion with modules for office automation, multi-media, and hypertext systems.
4. UNIX-based systems are becoming more popular.
5. Capability to work with databases on CD-ROM is becoming common.
6. Software packages are becoming more competitive in terms of price and facilities.

REFERENCES

1. G. Salton, *Automatic Text Processing—the Transformation, Analysis, and Retrieval of Information by Computer*, Reading, MA, Addison-Wesley Publishing Co. 1989.
2. J.E. Rowley, Guidelines on the Evaluation and Selection of Library Software Packages. *Aslib Proceedings*, 42(9), 1990, 225-235.

3. Pat Manson. Text Retrieval: Interfacing with Library Management Systems. In: R. Kimberley, *et. al.*, eds. Text Retrieval in Context. Proc. of the Institute of Information Scientists' Text Retrieval '84 Conf. London, Taylor Graham, 1984, pp. 138-144.
4. W. Saffady, *Text Storage and Retrieval Systems: a Technology Survey and Product Directory*, London, Meckler, 1989.
5. J. Leeves, *Library Systems: A Buyer's Guide*, Ed. 2, Aldershot, Gower, 1989.
6. H. Dyer and A. Gunson, *A Directory of Library and Information Retrieval Software for Microcomputers*, Ed. 4, Aldershot, Gower, 1990.
7. L.A. Tedd, *Introduction to Microcomputers for Libraries*, Ed. 3, Chichester, John Wiley, 1993.
8. G. Larsen, Library Automation in European Community Countries: an Overview. *Program*, 26(4), Oct. 1992, 361-371.
9. J.K. Bhargava, R.K. Srivastava and S.S. Murthy, SANJAY: an Indian Library automation package based on CDS/ISIS. *Program*, Vol. 27, No. 1, January 1993, pp. 51-66.
10. S. Chowdhury and G.G. Chowdhury. Development of Library management system using Micro-CDS/ISIS. *Annals of Library Science and Documentation*, Vol. 39, No. 3, 1992, pp. 113-122.
11. S. Chowdhury and G.G. Chowdhury. CIRC: a prototype circulation control system using Micro-CDS/ISIS, *IASLIC Bulletin*, 37(2), 1992, 73-81.
12. Calcutta Library Network (CALIBNET) Software: New Delhi Exposition a Curtain Raiser. *NISSAT Newsletter*, No. 3, 1991. 10-15.

Chapter 10
Text Retrieval and Library Management Software in India

10.1 INTRODUCTION

Although the world has gone far ahead in different areas of library automation, Indian libraries have yet to catch up. Some areas have been automated in a handful of libraries, but we have yet to have fully automated library system in the country. However, there has been a growing awareness of library automation and this has been enhanced by measures taken in various sectors vis-a-vis development of various software packages for library operations by various government and private agencies in the country. Different library network projects, *viz.*, the INFLIBNET (Information and Library Network of the University Grants Commission) at the national level, and regional library networks like BONET (Bombay Library Network), CALIBNET (Calcutta Library Network), DELNET (Delhi Library Network), MALIBNET (Madras Library Network), Poona Library Network *etc.*, are currently in progress and are likely to bring forth significant improvements in Indian library automation scenario.

Efforts in automating library catalogues and designing automated text retrieval systems in India have largely been influenced by the availability of the CDS/ISIS software from UNESCO through the NISSAT (National Information System in Science and Technology, a Government of India organisation). Increasing availability of training facilities in the package has also stimulated the interests of Indian library professionals towards the goal of automation.

Pending any published directory of indigenous text and library management software, it is difficult for library professionals to judge the value of any software that they are going to purchase. Software manufacturers and vendors often claim their products as the best in the market and claim that their software can act as a panacea. Discussions in this chapter concentrate on some common issues in the areas of text and library management software available in India.

Quite a few software for handling text retrieval and library management operations have been developed in India during the last few years. A list of such packages appear in Chapter 9. Out of the software mentioned in the list (Table 9.3), ten software packages (nine indigenous packages and Micro-CDS/ISIS) have been chosen to present a general overview of the features and facilities.

The discussions in this chapter do not aim to provide an exclusive review of the software packages. An attempt is made here to present some salient features of a few indigenous packages, and also to address some of the common problems in the areas of library automation in India.

10.2 CHOSEN PACKAGES

Nine indigenous packages and Micro-CDS/ISIS have been chosen to present an overview here. The nine indigenous packages are—CATMAN, LIBRARIAN, LibSys, MAITRAYEE, MECSYS, NIRMALS, SANJAY, TULIPS, and WILISYS. Though CDS/ISIS is not a software of Indian origin, it has been chosen because it is widely available to Indian libraries and, therefore, is being used in many libraries in one or more operations. The library management software SANJAY is based on the framework of CDS/ISIS and the aim of NISSAT is to make this package available to libraries along with CDS/ISIS to achieve an easy solution to the automation of both text retrieval and library housekeeping operations. The discussion in the following sections will address some of the major features of the chosen packages and thus will aim to assess their suitability to Indian libraries.

10.2.1 Genesis

Out of the ten packages chosen for this study, the reason for choosing CDS/ISIS has already been mentioned;

the other packages were chosen just to present a general idea about the activities going on in this area. Packages like SALIM (Software for Automation of Library and Information Management from Uptron India Ltd., Delhi)[1] (not discussed in this study) and WILISYS (WIPRO Library Information System from WIPRO India Ltd.)[2] were reported relatively earlier in comparison to the packages like CATMAN, LIBRARIAN, LibSys, MECSYS, NIRMALS, and TULIPS; the other two packages, *viz.*, MAITRAYEE and SANJAY are of more recent origin and are yet to make their way in the market.

Out of these packages, MAITRAYEE has been developed for a regional library network (viz., CALIBNET)[3], SANJAY has been developed on top of CDS/ISIS software by the DESIDOC Software team and has been patronised by a Government agency (*viz.*, NISSAT)[4-5], and CATMAN has also been developed by another Government agency (*viz.*, INSDOC, the Indian National Scientific Documentation Centre, a constituent establishment of the Council of Scientific and Industrial Research, Government of India). CDS/ISIS is also patronised by NISSAT while the other packages have been developed by commercial organisations. NIRMALS (Network of Information Resources and Management of Academic Library System) is developed by Nirmal Institute of Computer Expertise of Tiruchirapalli (Tamil Nadu), LIBRARIAN is developed by Soft-AID, a freelance software house of Pune, LibSys is the product of LibSys Corporation of Delhi, MECSYS is a product of MECON, Ranchi, TULIPS is a product of Tata Unisys Ltd., and WILISYS is from the WIPRO India Ltd.

10.3 BASIC FEATURES OF THE CHOSEN PACKAGES

So far there is no text retrieval system *per se* of Indian origin. Attempts have been made in some cases to develop such systems based on some DBMS/RDBMS packages, dBase IV for example, but with obvious limitations. Such systems lack, owing to the constraints of the underlying database management system, the versatility in handling and manipulation of textual data, as well as the desired retrieval facilities. CATMAN (Catalogue Management) chosen for this study has been developed on dBase IV; it uses fixed length field for handling textual data, and it does not provide much facilities as far as retrieval aspects are concerned. However, while using dBase as the underlying framework of text/information retrieval systems, some designers have attempted to overcome the problem of fixed length and repeatable fields and claim to achieve better performance (see for example, Mukhopadhayay).[6]

10.4 TEXT/INFORMATION RETRIEVAL FEATURES

Pending the availability of a suitable text retrieval system of Indian origin, many libraries have resorted to using CDS/ISIS for text and information retrieval purposes. However, there are other reasons for high usage of CDS/ISIS, the most prominent one is that it is available free-of-cost to non-profit organisations. The other reasons of course relate to the obvious advantages of this package, which briefly are

- it can be run on PC/XT onwards;
- it can hold a maximum of 16 million records;
- it allows variable length fields; allows subfields and repeatable fields;
- it allows online input and editing of data;
- data can be displayed and printed in a user-defined format;
- it allows creation of indexes of desired fields and the index file is organised as a B-tree;
- it has powerful search facilities; interactive searches can be conducted and search results can be saved;
- index terms can be displayed and a thesaurus can be used;
- it supports data import and export and data can be exchanged through the ISO 2709 format;
- data can be sorted by any desired key(s);
- a LAN (Local Area Network) version is available; and so on.

However, this package has also certain restrictions, particularly the search interface is not user-friendly and no online help is available. These issues are to be considered for further development of the package and measures suggested by Chowdhury[7-9] for this purpose may be taken into consideration.

SANJAY has been developed on the top of the CDS/ISIS framework for microcomputers in the MS-DOS environment (using the CDS/ISIS Pascal interface) and, therefore, it allows users to use the facilities of CDS/ISIS for text retrieval purposes while SANJAY can be used for library housekeeping jobs. However, SANJAY also provides a module for cataloguing which allows normal bibliographic information retrieval.

LibSys has been designed in C and therefore it does not suffer from the shortcomings of the underlying RDBMS framework for handling textual data as happens in case of the other software. This package is available in UNIX, XENIX, MS-DOS, as well as on LAN environment. LibSys provides text search and retrieval facilities in its 'Cataloguing' and 'Article Indexing and Abstracting' modules.

MAITRAYEE, developed for the CALIBNET has chosen INGRES as the underlying framework, while TULIPS has been developed on the top of ORACLE. Both these systems work in the UNIX environment and have been augmented with some programs written in C.

Similar is the case with MECSYS and WILISYS which have been developed on the top of UNIFY and work in the UNIX and XENIX environment.

The two other packages, *viz.*, NIRMALS and LIBRARIAN have been designed for the MS-DOS environment and they have been designed on the top of CLIPPER and FOXBASE, respectively. The packages are also available in LAN versions.

None of these packages has given much emphasis on text retrieval operations as such, but they provide facilities for basic search and retrieval operations in the cataloguing module. Some packages also provide additional modules for basic information retrieval purposes. For example, there are separate 'Search and Query' and 'Retrospective Search' modules in WILISYS, LibSys provides a separate 'Article Indexing and Abstracting' module, LIBRARIAN provides a separate module for 'Bibliographic Services', and MECSYS provides modules for 'Retrospective Search' and 'Information Dissemination'.

10.5 DATA INPUT

So far as the input of data is concerned, the packages offer facilities for entering data in a desired format. Some packages allow to adopt more than one format for data entry, for example, LibSys allows data entry in AACR2, CCF, or MARC format, NIRMALS, allows data entry in AACR2 and ISBD format, and so on. However, not all the packages provide adequate facilities for downloading of data and data exchange facilities. SANJAY, being based on CDS/ISIS, allows data exchange via ISO 2709 format; WILISYS also allows data exchange through ISO 2709 format. LibSys allows data conversion from CDS/ISIS and dBase. In other cases, separate program modules are necessary for import of data available in other format.

In relation to the question of nature of fields, packages which are based on a conventional database management framework have some obvious shortcomings. For example, packages based on ORACLE use long fields for longer data fields and therefore face some problems in creating index files.

Another major problem relates to the use of repeatable fields which are quite common in bibliographic/text databases. Some designers have resorted to the primitive approaches of using Author1, Author2, or Keyword1, Keyword2, *etc.* However, these problems did not arise in case of SANJAY because these facilities are available in CDS/ISIS. LibSys, being developed in C language has also taken care of variable length and repeatable fields. However, owing to the nature and size of the index files, the chosen packages will vary largely in their performance figures with a large text/bibliograpic database.

10.6 SCREEN FEATURES AND HELP

The packages under study have attempted to achieve good qualities of screen display and these have largely been possible by the available facilities in the underlying RDBMSs, except for SANJAY and LibSys where separate subroutines had to be developed for the purpose of screen handling.

The chosen packages also provide facilities for producing reports in a number of desired ways and these again have largely been facilitated by the underlying RDBMS frameworks. The chosen packages, except SANJAY and CDS/ISIS, provides good help facilities but none of the packages provide good online tutorial facilities which would have made the packages more user-friendly.

10.7 HOUSEKEEPING OPERATIONS

While CATMAN provides facilities only for catalogue management in libraries of small to medium sizes (with a collection of upto 50,000 documents), all the other packages (except CDS/ISIS) can handle normal library housekeeping operations like acquisition, cataloguing, circulation, and serials control (not available in SANJAY[4-5]).

Each package provides a number of modules for performing the various activities coming under each housekeeping operation. In general, the following facilities are provided by the packages for acquisition, circulation, and serials control:

Acquisition : Request checking, vendor selection, processing and generation of order, order monitoring, budget control, queries and report generation relating to status of an order, issue of reminders, status of fund, *etc.*

Circulation: Issue, return and reservation of books, maintenance of membership records, issue of reminders and notices, maintenance of transaction records, circulation queries, *etc.*

Serials Control: Monitoring of journal receipt, issue of reminders, renewal of journals, fund control, circulation of current issues, binding information, *etc.*

In addition, some packages provide facilities for additional information retrieval operations in libraries, like CAS and/or SDI (available in MECSYS, NIRMALS, WILISYS; it is also possible in SANJAY not as a module in it but as a provision in CDS/ISIS itself); OPAC interface (available in LibSys, NIRMALS, *etc.*), and so on.

MAITRAYEE, being developed for a library network programme provides specific network and communication facilities using TCP/IP as the communication software with X.25 protocol. Other packages do not provide communication facilities in the same way but either LAN version or multi-user environment is available, latter being the case for those which work in UNIX environment. The only exception is SANJAY which has been developed on version 2.3 of CDS/ISIS.[4-5] However, it is believed that the same can be used in a LAN environment provided version 3.0 onwards of CDS/ISIS (the formal network version) is used (see for discussion Chowdhury.[7-9])

10.8 PROBLEMS AND PROSPECTS

Major problems of library automation in India can be categorised into three major groups, *viz.*, funds, manpower, and retrospective conversion of databases. Due to economic recession in the country, libraries are hard pressed in their budget. For public libraries, with their limited funds, automation is still a difficult task. Very few academic and special libraries can afford the huge initial expenditure necessary for total automation.

Regarding the question of manpower, it can be stated that although India produces a significantly large number of trained post-graduate librarians every year, in most cases the candidates are not conversant with the environment of automation. Measures taken by the government and the employers in the country to alleviate the problem by providing short-term in-service training facilities, particularly in the areas of library automation, have proved to be quite successful but the total workforce is too large in comparison to the facilities available at the present moment.

The third point, that is, retrospective conversion of databases is a major issue in going for automation. In most cases, due to shortage of staff, library professionals find it difficult to cope with their normal day-to-day work, and therefore cannot think of devoting much time in retrospective database creation. Availability of readymade databases for downloading could alleviate much of these problems.

The packages under study vary greatly in terms of cost. While the cheapest one is CATMAN costing only Rs. 5,800 (remember this is only a package for cataloguing of books, and does not solve the problems of library automation as a whole), the maximum cost can go upto two million rupees or above (as in the case of MECSYS and TULIPS; of course this includes cost of the software, hardware, network nodes, training and other expertise). Price of other packages vary from Rs. 10,000 (for NIRMALS) to nearly 1,00,000 (for LibSys; of course Micro-LibSys costs Rs. 18,000).

Library housekeeping operations call for database management activities in libraries and, therefore, most of the packages have been developed on the top of RDBMS frameworks. However, packages which use RDBMSs as the underlying framework are bound to cost more altogether because end-users have to pay for both the library management software as well as for the underlying RDBMSs, the latters themselves being quite expensive as far as the Indian market is concerned. In this respect, packages developed from the scratch using a 3GL have clear advantages in making their ways in the market.

Performance of the packages in providing all the facilities, mentioned in the previous sections, in a library of reasonable size is however a question to be considered carefully and feedback from practising librarians will provide actual figures. An expert committee may be appointed to evaluate the various software packages available in the country. An attempt should also be made to produce a directory of indigenous software packages for handling library and information works. Such a directory should include basic features of each package, along with the merits and limitations so that librarians can have some general information about the available packages.

Although the ongoing projects for developing various library networks linking libraries in different parts of the country are promising signs for the library automation scenario, the professionals engaged in these projects should pay due attention to some important points. It has been noticed that each network project is choosing a different software as a basic framework for developing the network software. There is no standard guideline for the purpose. Again, the projects differ in choosing bibliographic formats for creation of their databases.

These are some of the most important factors, and unless a common practice is followed, these will cause problems in coordination and in sharing the resources among the various networks. Because different software is being developed for different network protects, libraries participating in different networks may have to develop interface programs for mutual access to databases. Similar problems will occur in exchange of data; conversion programs would be required to convert records from one bibliographic format to the other before they are downloaded.

Keeping in view the economic constraints of majority libraries, CDS/ISIS along with SANJAY has a very good prospect for automation of text retrieval and library management operations.[10] However, there are a couple of points of concern. The first one relates to the shortcoming of CDS/ISIS itself in relation to the search interface and online help facilities which need to be sorted out by the UNESCO software team engaged in developing the software. The second point relates to the underlying index file organisation of CDS/ISIS which very much dictates the function of the resulting library management software. The designers of the package have not clearly mentioned how would they handle aspects of the inverted file management (particularly its updating) in CDS/ISIS within the SANJAY software.[4-5] The other point relates to the possibilities of using the software on LAN. These issues have been addressed by Chowdhury in a recent research.[9] If adequate measures are taken, CDS/ISIS together with SANJAY in a LAN environment might prove to be the cheapest solution to the problems of library automation in India. Other software available now in India emphasize more on management of housekeeping operations rather than text retrieval aspects. Hence, choice of any such package may restrict text retrieval operations to some extent. However, as mentioned earlier in this book, choice of a particular software is dependent on the specific requirements and available resources of a library, and these should be the driving factors in choosing the appropriate software.

REFERENCES

1. News and events. *NISSAT Newsletter*, Vol. 6, No. 3, July-Sept. 1987, pp. 29.
2. WILISYS Software for Library computerisation. *NISSAT Newsletter*, Vol. 7, No. 2, Apr-June 1988, pp. 4-7.
3. Calcutta Library Network (CALIBNET) Software: New Delhi Exposition a Curtain Raiser. *NISSAT Newsletter*, Vol. 10, No. 3, July-Sept. 1991, 10-15.
4. DESIDOC Software Team. SANJAY: Augmented CDS/ISIS Package for Library Automation. *NISSAT Newsletter*, Vol. 10, No. 3, July-Sept. 1991, 3-6.
5. J.K. Bhargava, R.K. Srivastava and S.S. Murthy, SANJAY: an Indian Library Automation Package based on CDS/ISIS. *Program*, Vol. 27, No. 1, January 1993, 51-66.
6. A. Mukhopadhyay. Experimental Design of a Bibliographic Database with Variable Structure Field Length for dBase 3+ Applications. *IASLIC Bulletin*, Vol. 36, No. 2, 1991, 69-76.
7. S. Chowdhury and G.G. Chowdhury. Development of Library Management System using Micro-CDS/ISIS. *Annals of Library Science and Documentation*, Vol. 39, No. 3, 1992, 113-122.
8. S. Chowdhury and G.G. Chowdhury. CIRC: a Prototype Circulation Control System using Micro-CDS/ISIS. *IASLIC Bulletin*, Vol. No. 372, 1992, 73-81.
9. S. Chowdhury. *Applicability of the CDS/ISIS Package in the Automation of University Libraries With Particular Reference to India*, M. Phil Thesis, University of Sheffield, 1992.
10. G.G. Chowdhury and S. Chowdhury. Text Retrieval and Library Management Software in India, *Program*, Vol. 28, No. 3, July 1994, 253-261.

Chapter 11
Knowledge-based Systems

11.1 INTRODUCTION

Through our discussions so far we have come across the concepts of text/information retrieval systems, database management systems, and library management systems. With the advancement in information technology, artificial intelligence and expert systems, a new concept has come up which aims at incorporating knowledge about the domain and thus aims at handling knowledge rather than mere data. Such systems are called knowledge-based systems. The basic idea is to incorporate a set of rules into the system which will help to create some kind of knowledge base. These database systems are user-friendly, intelligent and responsive.

11.2 KNOWLEDGE-BASED SYSTEMS

Knowledge-based systems (KBSs) refer to those kinds of systems where knowledge specific to the domain is stored in such a way that it can be used by the system for retrieving information in response to a particular request, or to arrive at a decision, whenever necessary. In KBSs, knowledge of the problem (domain knowledge) is embedded in the instructions which tells the computer how to process the knowledge. Using knowledge-based methodology the correctness of the domain knowledge can easily be checked, the knowledge can be easily changed and effects of changes can be monitored easily.

Many types of rule need to be stored in a knowledge base, for example[1]

— defining constraints on domain and attribute values;
— defining integrity and consistency constraints;
— deriving new data;
— defining user views;
— categorisation or defining subsets;

— specifying the characteristic of relationships;
— defining partitions in a distributed database; *etc.*

These kinds of knowledge can be incorporated into the system by any of the available means for incorporating semantic information into a system, like semantic net, production rules, conceptal dependency, frames, *etc.*[2-6]

11.3 RELATED AREAS

Knowledge-based systems also need intelligent user interfaces. In traditional DBMS or text/information retrieval systems, it is usually presumed that users will be able to formulate the appropriate search strategy for each and every query. This is too optimistic an attitude; in practice, the system often fails to produce desired result due to ill-framed query. Intelligent user interfaces are produced to overcome this problem. In such systems, users are required to present their query as simply as possible. The system will be intelligent enough to make out the specific requirement of the given user; it may often lead the user to some sort of question-answer session at the end of which the system generates the appropriate search expression.

One of the key areas to the development of KBSs, and consequently the intelligent user interfaces, is the language. Much research has been done in the recent past in natural language processing and its application to different areas of information retrieval, thus giving rise to a number of automatic systems for text and information retrieval.[7-9]

11.4 USES OF KBSs

KBSs can be used in different areas of LIS (Library and Information Science) activities. Ford[6] maintains that KBSs are relevant to library and information professionals in that they can help

1. achieve traditional LIS in-house objectives more cost-effectively;
2. offer clients new types of knowledge resource; and
3. develop the professional role of library and information personnel.

Travis[10] identifies four areas where KBSs can be used in information work, for example:

1. The use of KBSs for reference and referral;
2. The use of KBSs to improve Online Public Access Catalogues (OPACs);
3. The use of KBSs to improve end-user searching of specialised bibliographic databases with controlled vocabularies; and
4. The use of KBSs to improve end-user text searching.

Examples of some Knowledge-based systems which are used in different areas of library and information activities are provided in the following subsections.

11.4.1 Indexing

Reuter's TIS (Topic Identification System) is a KBS that indexes news stories automatically. The TCS (Text Categorisation Shell) developed as part of TIS can be used for text retrieval, routing messages and indexing large texts, such as maintenance manuals[11]. Another system for automatic indexing using knowledge-based techniques is the MedIndEx. It is developed at the National Library of Medicine, Bethesda, USA, to assist indexers in selecting index terms and applying the indexing rules associated with the MeSH (Medical Subject Headings) system.[12]

11.4.2 Front-end Systems

The potential of KBSs in text and database searching for better retrieval is an area that has received a great deal of attention. One of the most cited specialised interfaces for end-user searching is CANSEARCH which helps users with the technicalities of formulating a MEDLINE search.[13]

TOME.SEARCHER is a commercially available intelligent front-end to databases, designed to facilitate online searching activities; TOME.SELECTOR is another system designed to recommend which of some 1,000 databases of the main host services available from the Tom Associates are relevant to the enquirer's needs.[14] EURISKO is another front-end system which[15]

— facilitates information access to online databases by unskilled users, and
— relieves skilled intermediaries of the need for detailed technical knowledge of unfamiliar databases.

11.4.3 Reference Services

Providing guidance to reference materials is an area which has several points that distinguishes it from other applications. The Answerman system at the National Agricultural Library (NAL) gives prominence to solve specific questions or problems.[16] Another system for providing automatic aids to users in reference service is PLEXUS.[17] Answerman and PLEXUS present a contrast in focus: Answerman has more scope but very limited knowledge-based capabilities, while PLEXUS has more power but very limited subject matter.[10] RADA (Research and Development Advisor) is another system which is designed to be used by researchers in a research and development environment. This system helps users formulate information requests, employ knowledge about users' research interests to help the research process, and suggests interesting lines of research using knowledge of the subject and of users' interests.[18]

11.4.4 Content Analysis and Information Retrieval

The SIMPR (Structured Information Management: Processing and Retrieval) project is a program of research between academic and industrial partners in Scotland, Denmark, Finland, Portugal, Ireland and the Netherlands, with an objective of applying natural language, expert systems and machine learning techniques to different aspects of information retrieval.[19]

SCISOR (System for Conceptual Information Summarization, Organisation and Retrieval) is an information retrieval system that reads news stories about mergers and acquisitions from a newswire source (online financial news from Dow Jones), extracts information from the stories, and answers questions in English pertaining to what it has read.[20-21] SCISOR runs on a Sun workstation and it processes news at the rate of six stories per minute.[22] A test result shows that out of one day's total of 729 stories, SCISOR achieved over 90% averaged recall and precision in its determination of which stories were about merger and acquisitions. It correctly identified the target and suitor in 90% of all the stories. When dollar-per-share values were present in the stories, SCISOR extracted this quantity in 79% of the cases, and the total value of the offer in 82% cases.[23]

Another system, designed to answer question, is RESEARCHER which[22]

- — analyses patent abstracts and creates a knowledge base;
- — searches for similarities between different patents, and adds the generalisations to the memory;
- — answers questions, including questions requiring the use of information derived for more than any single abstract; and
- — customizes its answers for different types of enquiry.

RESEARCHER is intended to accept information presented in natural language form, in particular, patent abstracts. It analyses patent abstracts and creates a knowledge representation of the information they contain; it can search for similarities between different patents and it answers questions about the information in the memory.

The research group 'Systemes Intelligents de Recherches d'Information' of the 'Laboratoire Genie Informatique de Grenoble' is pursuing a programme aimed at developing a system which will automatically construct and update a knowledge base, to be used in information retrieval, by analysing natural language texts in a particular domain.[24-25]

The TINA (Text-Inhalts-Analyse: text content analysis) project,[26] developed at the Siemens Corporate Research Laboratories in Germany, aims at developing natural language processing software for information retrieval, free-text searching and indexing, automatic abstracting, thesaurus building and natural language search question input for textual databases. The application areas are the commercial free-text databases on mainframes as well as the field of text handling on a personal computer.[26-28] The TINA project was started in the mid-eighties, based on more than five years of previous research and development work in information and documentation. The TINA software has been tested by the US Department of Commerce for patent search and indexing.[28]

The TINA research and development work is focused on Syntactical analysis for full-text documents and large free-text databases. The syntactic analysis in TINA first isolates noun phrases in a text. A number of syntactic rules help to build the dependency structure of the isolated noun phrases. The syntactic processing of texts thus results in structures where dependency relations between words are made explicit. By evaluating these relations for all the words of a database statistically, each text word is correlated with all other words by which it is determined/specified or which it determines/specifies itself. This exercise helps in building the 'syntactic tables' for the database words. Syntactic tables can be used for searching and indexing free text databases. It can also be used in order to match multi-word expressions against full text documents.

The users of this system submit phrases to the text and get more and more detailed ideas about the content of the full text document. The syntactic analysis is done by an automatic search and indexing system called COPSY (Context OPerator SYntax), which performs a number of functions, *viz.*, automatic noun phrase recognition, noun phrase selection, noun phrase normalization, noun phrase matching, and automatic document ranking on the basis of syntactic criteria.[28] The rules that determine the syntactic links are formulated in terms of various syntactic categories like noun, adverb, preposition, *etc.*

The processing of 195,000 abstracts from the USPTO (United States Patent and Trademark Office) resulted in 140 MB of 'dependency structures'[26]. The TINA evaluation was performed on the basis of 50 PTO abstracts which were not involved in rule development and which belonged to different patent domains. The syntactic analysis resulted in 85% recall and 84% precision.[26]

11.5 SHELLS AND TOOLS

Nowadays a number of tools for building KBSs are available for personal computers which allow non-programmers to build systems easily. Such tools are called 'shells'. They typically comprise a friendly userinterface, a knowledge representation language, which defines rules for the knowledge base, and an inference engine which uses expert knowledge to solve problems by 'reasoning'. Thus, shells are basically KBSs stripped of their domain knowledges. Users are provided guidelines for easy building of a new system by adding a new knowledge base. The idea is that knowledge from an expert or several experts can be collected and searched by a programmer and entered into an empty expert system's shell. Rules and relationships about the knowledge can then be applied, allowing the non-experts to question the knowledge base which will come up with reasonable answers.

The most popular platform for expert systems shells is the IBM-compatible PC, but mini-and mainframe computers from DEC and IBM follow closely.[6] In simpler shells the rules will consist of rules and facts; more sophisticated shells allow the use of, for example, frames and inheritance, and/or ways of handling uncertainty. A number of expert systems shells are now available. Richard Barron[29] provides a list of 34 expert system shells which were available in the UK market in early 1989. These shells have been designed for a wide range of computing environments; they provide facilities for performing a number of tasks and price tags range from less than £ 100 to over 3,000. Some of these shells are particularly useful for text/information retrieval purposes.

Level 5 from Information Builders run on PC/XTs, ATs, and Apple Mac. It is described as an expert systems shell with English-like syntax and online help system. Special application environment of Level 5 includes decision management, diagnostics, scheduling, text handling, intelligent text processing, process monitoring, etc.

Similarly, KnowledgePro from Knowledge Garden (Intellisoft UK Ltd.) is designed for hypertext, list processing, and interfaces to other languages and programmes. KnowledgePro integrates hypertext and expert systems; it stores knowledge in natural chunks called topics. KnowledgePro database toolkit allows user to read in dBase and Lotus 1-2-3 files from within knowledgePro, and graphics toolkit allows images to be linked with text or data.

11.6 CONCLUSION

KBSs and more specifically IKBSs (Intelligent Knowledge-based Systems) have brought a new dimension to the process of information handling and management. Many information retrieval operations, which were earlier thought to be impossible to perform without the 'intellectual involvement' of human being, can now be performed with the help of IKBSs. However, most of the tools available to date work at a fairly low level; large operational systems are still in the process of improvement.

Lancaster, quoting Metzler,[30] suggests that

> 'The library of the future may be able to. provide a far richer access to, and utilization of, the knowledge contained (often simplicity) in its collection. The most immediately feasible development along this line would be content-based information retrieval. This, of course, would require a far more general and robust brand of artificial intelligence and natural language understanding than what we have available now.'

Continuous research in different areas of information technology, natural language processing, image processing, expert systems, and artificial intelligence, are bridging the gap between the dreams and practical possibilities,[31] and thus altogether are leading us to library of the future, which, according to Feigenbaum *et.al.*,[32] should be an 'active, intelligent knowledge server'.

REFERENCES

1. E. Oxborrow, *Databases and Database Systems: Concepts and Issues*, London, Chartwell-Bratt, 1989.
2. E. Charniak and D. McDermott, *Introduction to Artificial Intelligence*, Reading, MA, Addison-Wesley, 1985.
3. A. Barr and E.A. Feigenbaum, eds., *Handbook of Artificial Intelligence*, London, Pitman, 1981.
4. R. Schank and R. Ableson, *Scripts, Plans, Goals, and Understanding*, Hillsdale, NJ, Lawrence Erlbaum Assoc., 1977.

5. R.J. Brachman and D.L. McGuiness. Knowledge Representation, Connectionism, and Conceptual Retrieval. In: 11th International Conference on Research and Development in Information Retrieval, Greenoble, France, 1988. Washington, Association of Computing Machinery, 1988, pp. 161-174.
6. N. Ford, *Expert Systems and Artificial Intelligence: an Information Manager's Guide*, London, Library Association, 1991.
7. G.G. Chowdhury, Natural Language Processing and Information Retrieval. Part 1: Basic issues. *IASLIC Bulletin*, 36(2), 1991, 45-49.
8. G.G. Chowdhury, Natural Language Processing and Information Retrieval. Part 2: Major Applications. *IASLIC Bulletin*, 36(2), 1991, 51-59.
9. G.G. Chowdhury, *Application of Natural Language Processing to Chemical Patents*, PhD Thesis, University of Sheffield, UK, 1992.
10. I.L. Travis. Knowledge-based Systems in Information Work: a View of the Future. In: C. Roysdon and H.D. White, eds. Expert System in Reference Services. New York, Haworth Press, 1989, pp. 41-60.
11. P.J. Hays and S.P. Weinstein, CONSTRUE/TIS: a System for Content-based Indexing of a Database of News Stories. In: Proc. of the Second Annual Conf. on Innovative Applications of Artificial Intelligence, Georgetown University, Washington DC, 1990.
12. S.M. Humphrey, MedIndEx System: Medical Indexing Expert System. *Information Processing and Management*, 25(1), 1989, 73-88.
13. S. Pollitt. CANSEARCH: an Expert Systems Approach to Document Retrieval. *Information Processing and Management*, 23(2), 1987, 119-138.
14. A. Durham, Having the Last Word on Information Retrieval. *Computing*, 18 May, 1990, 32-33.
15. C. Barthes and P. Glize. Planning in an Expert System for Automated Information Retrieval. In: Y. Chiaramella, ed. Proc. of the Eleventh International ACM-SIGIR Conf. on Research and Development in Information Retrieval, Grenoble, France, June 13-15, 1988. New York, ACM, 1988, pp. 535-549.
16. S.T. Waters, Answerman, the Expert Information Specialists: an Expert System for Retrieval of Information from Library Reference Books. *Information Technology and Library*, 5(3), 1986, 204-212.

17. A. Vickery and H.M. Brooks. PLEXUS: the Expert System for Referral. *Information Processing and Management*, 23(2), 1987, 99-117.
18. T.C. Tan, P. Smith and M. Pegman. RADA: an Intelligent Research and Development Advisor. *Expert Systems for Information Management*, 2(2), 1989, 81-104.
19. A. Smeaton. SIMPR: Using Natural Language Processing Techniques for Information Retrieval. In: A. S. Pollitt, ed. Proc. of the Twelfth BCS IRSG Research Colloquium on Information Retrieval, Huddersfield, April 3-4, 1990. London, British Computer Society Information Retrieval Specialist Group, 1990, pp. 152-161.
20. L.F. Rau and P.S. Jacobs, Integrating Top-down and Bottom-up Strategies in a Text Processing System. In: Proceedings of the 2nd Conference on Applied Natural Language Processing. 1988, pp. 129-135.
21. L.F. Rau. Knowledge Organisation and Access in a Conceptual Information System. *Information Processing and Management*, 23, 1987, 269-283.
22. P.S. Jacobs and L.F. Rau. SCISOR: Extracting Information from On-line News. *Communications of the ACM*, 33, 1990. 88-97.
23. M. Lebowitz. An Experiment in Intelligent Information Systems: RESEARCHER. In: R. Davies, ed. Intelligent Information Systems: Progress and Prospects. Chichester, Ellis Horwood, 1986, pp. 127-49.
24. M.F. Bruandet. Outline of a Knowledge-base Model for an Intelligent Information Retrieval System. *Information Processing and Management*, 25(1), 1989, 89-115.
25. Y. Chairamella and B. A. Defude. A Prototype of an Intelligent System for Information Retrieval: IOTA. *Information Processing and Management*, 23(4), 1987, 285-303.
26. G. Ruge, C. Schwarz and A. J. Warner. Effectiveness and Efficiency in Natural Language Processing for Large Amounts of Text. *Journal of the American Society for Information Science*, 42, 1991, 450-456.
27. C. Schwarz. Content Based Text Handling. *Information Processing and Management*, 26, 1990, 219-226.
28. C. Schwarz. Automatic Syntactic Analysis of Free Text. *Journal of the American Society for Information Science*, 41, 1990, 408-417.
29. Richard Barron. Great Expectations: Expert Systems Shell Survey. *Systems International*, April 1989, 35-40.
30. D.P. Metzler. Artificial Intelligence: What Will They Think

for Next? In: Artificial Intelligence and Expert Systems: Will They Change the Library? Proceedings of the 27th Annual Clinic on Library Applications of Data Processing. ed. by F.W. Lancaster and L.C. Smith. Urbana, University of Illinois, Graduate School of Library and Information Science, pp. 3-49. *Quoted in,* F.W. Lancaster. Artificial Intelligence and Expert Systems: How Will They Contribute? In: F.W. Lancaster, ed. Libraries and the Future: Essays on the Library in the Twenty-First Century. New York, The Haworth Press, 1993, pp. 147-156.

31. Anne Morris, ed., *The Application of Expert Systems in Libraries and Information Centres.* London, Bowker-Saur, 1992.
32. E. Feigenbaum and P. McCorduck and H.P. Nii, *The Rise of the Expert Company,* London, Macmillan, 1988.

Chapter 12
Recent Studies and Trends in Text Retrieval

12.1 INTRODUCTION

Automated text retrieval systems are in use for more than the past three decades. There have been manifold developments in the text retrieval environment during this period. The first application of computers in text/information retrieval was in the area of generation of keyword indexes. This was the beginning of the beginning. Different libraries and institutions then invested much efforts in the creation of automated catalogues of books and other reading materials for in-house use as well as for online searching, All these systems were, in the strict sense of the term, reference or bibliographic retrieval systems; what these systems were retrieving at the end of a search session was not any kind of text but information about texts. However, significant efforts were made from the beginning to improve the retrieval performance by devising many boolean and non-boolean retrieval mechanisms. Retrieval features available in most text retrieval systems today, described in Chapters 4 and 6 in this book, are results of this research.

Side by side efforts were made to retrieve the actual text at the end of a search by incorporating abstract and/or full text in the system. Such efforts called for further research in the development of retrieval mechanisms so as to make the retrieval features suitable for full text systems. Creation of full text databases is always a labour-intensive and time-consuming task. Optical Character Recognition (OCR) technology appeared as a solution (although not fully and not without faults) to the problem.

New developments in database technology, particularly application of some new mechanisms and scientific principles to the design and development of databases, also had a significant effect on the development of text retrieval systems. The other significant development in the area took place when efforts were made to include non-textual materials, such as images, within the text retrieval environment. This called for significant research since efficient handling (storage and retrieval) of images itself is a complex area of research.

There have also been significant developments in another area, *viz.*, human-computer interface design, which contributes to the ease of using text retrieval systems. Efforts have been made to improve user interfaces and to make them more friendly so that end-users can approach the text retrieval systems more easily and can interact in natural language as far as practicable. Developments have also taken place in automatic processing of texts over the past few years. Researchers are trying to overcome the problems caused by simple keyword indexing which is the basis of retrieval of most text retrieval systems even today. New mechanisms have been devised recently for automatic categorisation, analysis, interpretation and representation of large amounts of text without human intervention.

Thus, there are many areas of research and experimentation which have contributed to the development of text retrieval systems over the years. Some of the current studies and research in different areas of text and information retrieval have been highlighted in this chapter in order to show the trend. Some novel approaches to the process of design and development of text databases have been mentioned followed by a brief discussion on some recent studies in different areas of information retrieval like

— a new look at the parameters for measuring retrieval effectiveness like recall and precision,
— suitability of the OCR technology in the creation of full text databases,
— automatic text categorisation and term extraction processes,
— comparison of boolean and ranked retrieval mechanisms,
— natural language user interfaces, *etc.*

Finally, the prospect of text retrieval systems has been highlighted with a brief discussion on one of the major shortcomings of information retrieval experiments and the recent measures taken to alleviate that problem.

12.2 INTEGRATED DATABASES

Some applications of text retrieval systems call for the creation of integrated databases. An information support system should have databases of bibliographic records, personal and institutional records, project records, and so on. Such an information system should be able to retrieve bibliographic records as well as records of persons and institutions and on-going/completed projects in a given area. If separate databases for bibliographic, personal/ institutional and project records are created, users have to conduct separate search in each database.

One objective of designing integrated databases is to reduce the number of searches to be carried out in different databases of similar kind. Neelameghan[1] shows that a single search in an integrated database system, designed using mini-micro CDS/ISIS, can retrieve records related to all the bibliographic, personal/institutional and project records available in the database. Abebe *et.al*[2] have reported the creation and use of an integrated database, named ABNCD, using Micro-CDS/ISIS, which consists of bibliographic records, and profiles of institutions, information systems, projects and experts.

12.3 SYSTEMATIC APPROACHES TO DEVELOPING INFORMATION SYSTEMS

Information system methodologies have proved invaluable in the development of information systems. Implementation of a library management system involves considerable work to be conducted in the selection of an appropriate system, and tailoring of that system to suit the local needs. Jennifer Rowley[3] outlines a systems methodology for the selection and implementation of library management systems. Methodology for the selection and implementation of library management systems offered by Rowley[3] involves five major stages, *viz.*

(1) Definition of objectives,
(2) Specification of the requirements,
(3) Systems selection,
(4) Systems implementation, and
(5) Systems evaluation.

Neelameghan[4] shows applications of the postulates, principles and techniques formulated by Dr. S.R. Ranganathan, within the framework of his general theory of classification, at various stages in the development of text databases: in conceptualising, structuring and organising information as perceived by specialist users and preparing databases therefrom. It is suggested that the postulates, principles and techniques of the general theory of classification can be used to

- organising concepts and structuring databases;
- preparing field definition table/data dictionary for databases;
- assisting user to browse more conveniently in the databases;
- analysing facets of user's query and structuring search expressions for better results in retrieval; and
- presenting the retrieved records in a sequence helpful to users.

12.4 FOCUSES OF CURRENT RESEARCH AND DEVELOPMENT

Jennifer Rowley[5] mentions that the major focuses for development in text retrieval systems in the recent years have been in areas of

- human-computer interface design;
- integration with other systems;
- designing open systems;
- image handling; and
- optical character recognition.

Recall and precision, recall-precision plots in particular, have been used for many years to characterise performance of information retrieval systems. Empirical studies of retrieval performance have shown a tendency for precision to decline as recall increases.[6] Buckland and Gay[7] have recently studied the relationship between recall and precision conceptually to delineate the theoretical limits to retrieval performance in terms of "benchmark" retrieval behaviours. It has been noted that with large databases and/or information systems there can be advantages to retrieval in two (or more) stages: initial retrieval emphasizing high recall, followed by more detailed searching of the initial retrieved set, can be used to improve both recall and precision simultaneously, though the trade-off between recall and precision cannot be avoided altogether.

Accessing data, particularly full text, in a form directly usable by an information retrieval system is quite difficult. Manual creation of data by keyboarding is extremely slow and expensive. The transition from printed document to ASCII format is a crucial component, and performance of the retrieval systems depends largely on the accuracy of the process. Optical character recognition (OCR) technology is an important tool for overcoming the problem. In recent years OCR vendors have made vast improvements in their commercial products; some vendors claim 99% character accuracy. As high as this accuracy seems, there could still be upto 25 misspelled words per page. Thus, a text database created using the best OCR technology available in the market could have noisy data. Manual correction of this data is costly and time-intensive.

Taghva *et. al*[8] attempted to determine what effect errors in optically recognized documents will have on retrieval and whether the manual correction step can be avoided while achieving a reasonable rate of retrieval effectiveness. Results of preliminary tests indicate that at least in an environment where 100% accuracy is not imperative, OCR and information retrieval can be applied in succession with little or no human intervention. However, this experiment has not taken some other factors into consideration, like how will the added overhead, caused by unnecessary increase in the size of the inverted file due to inclusion of some misspelled words and graphic text, affect the performance of the system, how will the users confidence be affected by the noisy data, and so on. When these issues are properly addressed within large text retrieval systems, OCR technology may be practised more confidently in the creation of text databases.

It has been noted by researchers some time ago that the keyword-level searching facilities offered by text retrieval systems are inadequate in many respects. The basic assumption in designing the search interfaces of most of the commercially available text retrieval systems have been that users are able to express their information requirements by choosing the appropriate search terms and they are able to arranging those terms logically, by using the appropriate boolean operators, to prepare the search statement. However, it has been noted that the poor performance of text retrieval systems is often attributed to these assumptions which do not work in reality. Researchers have therefore been trying to design more and more user-friendly interfaces that are capable of guiding users in formulating their search statements, and in some cases accepting natural language queries and then producing the search statement internally that is acceptable by the corresponding text retrieval system. Some natural language user interfaces designed over the past few years show promising results.[9] Similar systems designed for automatic analysis and interpretation of texts in natural language, commonly known as natural language text processing systems, have also brought new promises in text retrieval environment.[9] Graphical user interfaces and window-based user interfaces are also becoming increasingly common.

Information retrieval systems are not limited to texts only; text and images occur side by side and mechanisms for handling both the text and images are very much necessary. Some text retrieval systems have already introduced modules for image handling. The trend is to develop systems for successfully storing, processing and retrieving of documents in its entirety—text as well as images.[5]

The recent ACM-SIGIR conference[10] reports some exciting research in different areas of information retrieval. Automatic text categorisation is one of the major problem areas in text, particularly full text retrieval. Lewis and Gale[11] describe an approach called uncertainty sampling for automatic categorisation of texts. Yang[12] addresses a major problem in text categorisation which is caused by the vocabulary differences between user queries and documents and proposes a system called ExpNet which, with the capability of learning from human experiences, can solve the problem of vocabulary difference with a low computation cost. Apte, Dameru and Weiss[13] describe a methodology for automatic generation of text categorisation models which perform satisfactorily across large document collection in two languages (Reuter's English and German Newswires). Hoch[14] reports the INFOCLAS system which applies statistical methods of information retrieval for the classification of German business letters into corresponding message types such as order, offer, and so on.

A major aim of text retrieval systems is to present to users a sequence of documents ranked in decreasing order of query document similarities. Users are able to minimize their time spent to find useful information by consulting the top-ranking documents only. Although conventional boolean retrieval systems have advantages of easy implementation, they cannot rank documents in order of relevance. Extended boolean models such as Fuzzy set, Walker-Kraft, Paice, P-Norm, and Infinite-One have been developed to provide ranked output.[15] Lee[15] analyses the mathematical properties of the operators used in the extended boolean retrieval models and suggests that P-Norm is the most suitable for achieving high-recall effectiveness.

Turtle[16] reports a research in one of the most debated areas of text retrieval. He presents comparison of retrieval performance of boolean versus natural language searching in a large commercial system, called WESTLAW that provides access to US legal materials, and shows that natural language searching performs better for all of the material types tested. However, it is suggested that boolean query languages will not altogether disappear in the near future because for some kind of materials and some queries boolean techniques may be preferable and some users, due to their long acquaintance with the system, prefer boolean searching. At the same time for average user natural language query may give better results than boolean query.

Turtle[16] recommends that commercial systems will need to support both the query types; the performance difference can be noticeable over the time for there is a lot of room for improvement of current generation of natural language systems.

12.5 PROSPECTS

Text retrieval software incorporate retrieval features and mechanisms which are the product of sustained research of information scientists over the years. However, sometimes commercial software or database producers are skeptical about employing the results of these researches. A notable example is the fact that although experimental results reported in the 1970s[17] have shown that simple natural language query techniques are at least as effective as boolean techniques on comparable retrieval problems, major text retrieval systems offer only boolean search facilities even today.

Major reason of this trade-off is that most of the new retrieval mechanisms were tested with a small set of data and their performance in the real-life situation remained unanswered. According to Donna Harman, the Chair of the TREC (the Text Retrieval Conferences, TREC-1 and TREC-2), researchers in information retrieval have conducted research with collections like CACM, NPL, and INSPEC collections, each of the order of thousands of documents; this weakness alone has meant that information retrieval research of the last few decades could be accused of being small scale and consequently out of touch with reality.[18] Similar remarks have been made by Vickery and Vickery in a recent paper reviewing the state of research in designing online user interfaces:[19]

> 'Many of the interfaces discussed above have handled restricted subject domains. Others, though ranging much more widely, have not been thoroughly tested with a large set of input queries. There is a question mark over the robustness of many systems, in particular with regard to the two transformation: NLQ→ IQL; IQL→ SL that is, query processing to

create an internal query representation, and transformation of this into an appropriate search statement.'

These criticisms have been accepted by researchers on different occasions; but the major problem that they faced was the unavailability of large test collections and reliable (tested) retrieval measures. However, the situation is changing now; efforts are now being made to overcome this problem. In 1991, the US Defence Advanced Research Projects (DARPA) decided to fund the TREC experiments to be run by the National Institute of Science and Technology (NIST) in order to allow information retrieval researchers to scale up from small collections of data to larger experiments. The draft results of the TREC-1 experiments revealed that[18]

— automatic construction of queries from natural language query statements seems to work;

— techniques based on natural language processing were no better and no worse than those based on vector or probabilistic approaches; the best of each of the approaches are all about equal, *etc.*

After the experiments under the TREC initiatives are over (TREC-1 held in 1992, TREC-2 held in 1993, *etc.*), researchers in different fields of text and information retrieval will have a large collection of text documents (as much as two gigabytes of text), 100 test query topics and detailed relevance assesments.[18] When all these become publicly available, information retrieval research will be truly in touch with reality, and the results of this research will soon reach the end-users of text retrieval systems.

REFERENCES

1. A. Neelameghan, *Designing an integrated database using CDS/ISIS mini-micro version. A case study and brief guide to LIST: a prototype for an integrated database.* Paris, UNESCO, 1986.
2. Abebe Rorissa, B.B. Bamuhiiga, J. Chisenga, C.S. Nxumalo, D.A. Sekimang'a and A. Neelameghan, ABNCD+: a prototype for an integrated information storage and retrieval system. *Microcomputers for Information Management*, 9(3), 1992, 137-159.

3. Jennifer Rowley, Aspects of a library systems methodology. *Journal of Information Science,* 20(1), 1994, 41-45.
4. A. Neelameghan, Application of Ranganathan's general theory of knowledge classification in designing specialized databases. *Libri,* 42(3), July-Sept. 1992, 202-226.
5. Jennifer Rowley, *Computers for libraries,* London, Library Association, 1992.
6. C.W. Cleverdon, On the inverse relationship of recall and precision. *Journal of Documentation,* 28, 1972, 195-201.
7. Michael Buckland and Fredric Gay, The relationship between recall and precision. *Journal of the American Society for Information Science.* 45(1), 1994, 12-19.
8. K. Tagva, J. Brosack, Allen Condit and S. Erva, The effect of noisy data on text retrieval. *Journal of the American Society for Information Science,* 45(1), 1994, 50-58.
9. G.G. Chowdhury, *Information retrieval system,* Calcutta, Iaslic, 1994.
10. W. Bruce Croft and C.J. van Rijsbergen, eds. SIGIR '94: Proceedings of seventeenth ACM-SIGIR conference on research and development in information retrieval, Dublin, Ireland, July 3-6, 1994. London, Springer-Verlag, 1994.
11. D.D. Lewis and W.A. Gale, A sequential algorithm for training text classifiers. In: W. Bruce Croft and C.J. Van Rijsbergen, eds. SIGIR '94: Proceedings of seventeenth ACM-SIGIR conference on research and development in information retrieval, Dublin, Ireland, July 3-6, 1994. London, Springer-Verlag, 1994. pp. 3-12.
12. Y. Yang, Expert network: effective and efficient learning for human decisions in text categorisation and retrieval. In: W. Bruce Croft and C.J. van Rijsbergen, eds. SIGIR '94: Proceedings of seventeenth ACM-SIGIR conference on research and development in information retrieval, Dublin, Ireland, July 3-6, 1994. London, Springer-Verlag, 1994, pp. 13-21.
13. C. Apte, F. Dameru, S. Weiss, Towards language independent automated learning of text categorisation models. In: W. Bruce Croft and C.J. van Rijsbergen, eds. SIGIR '94: Proceedings of seventeenth ACM-SIGIR conference on research and development in information retrieval, Dublin, Ireland, July 3-6, 1994. London, Springer-Verlag, 1994. pp. 22-30.
14. R. Hoch, using IR techniques for text classification in document analysis. In: W. Bruce Croft and C.J. van Rijsbergen, eds. SIGIR '94: Proceedings of seventeenth ACM-

SIGIR conference on research and development in information retrieval, Dublin, Ireland, July 3-6, 1994. London, Springer-Verlag, 1994. pp. 31-40.

15. J.H. Lee, Properties of extended boolean models in information retrieval. In: W. Bruce Croft and C.J. van Rijsbergen, eds. SIGIR '94: Proceedings of seventeenth ACM-SIGIR conference on research and development in information retrieval, Dublin, Ireland, July 3-6, 1994. London, Springer-Verlag, 1994. pp. 182-190.
16. H. Turtle, Natural language vs. boolean query evaluation: a comparison of retrieval performance. In: W. Bruce Croft and C.J. van Rijsbergen, eds. SIGIR '94: Proceedings of seventeenth ACM-SIGIR conference on research and development in information retrieval, Dublin, Ireland, July 3-6, 1994. London, Springer-Verlag, 1994. pp. 212-220.
17. Karen Spark Jones, *Information retrieval experiment*, London, Butterworth, 1981.
18. Donna K. Harman, A special conference report: the first text retrieval conference (TREC-1), Rockville, MD, USA, 4-6 Nov. 1992. *Information Processing and Management*, 29(4), 1993, 411-414.
19. Brian Vickery and Alina Vickery, Online search interface design. *Journal of Documentation*, 49(2), June 1993, 103-187.

Index